CORRESPONDING
WITH
LEGENDS II

THIS TIME... IT'S FOOTBALL

CRAIG SIEVERS

Downtown
BOOKS
COFFEE
Auburn, NY

Cover photography by Craig Sievers and design by Ryan Z Bartlett.

For information on this title contact:
Downtown Books Publishing
66 Genesee Street
Auburn, NY 13021
downtownbooksandcoffee.com/

ISBN: 978-0-692-31865-2

TABLE OF CONTENTS

i

To Leanne,
for her unending love and support.

INTRODUCTION

Dear Reader,

If you have not yet read my first book I would like to explain where my passion for writing letters began. When I was six years old I began a lifelong enthusiasm for collecting sports cards. Later on, I began to send cards to players asking to get them signed. I included a question at the end of one of those letters to a former All Star baseball player with whom I share a last name. Roy Sievers signed a card for me and wrote me a full page letter telling me that he did not think we were related. It was then that I realized that the men I was writing were actually reading my letters and might be willing to write me in response.

The difference between this book and the last is the difference between baseball and football. Most everyone has or does play baseball or softball. Little league, gym class, sand lots, city leagues, church leagues, just about everybody has swung a bat at a pitched ball. Full contact football on the other hand is not something that everyone does. I, for instance never played football other than sandlot or in gym class. I was not big or strong enough and I never wanted to put in the work of two-a-day practices in the summer time heat. The coach at my high school asked me to come out for running back on the team, but there was not a lot of incentive for me to be a 5' 6", 145 lb. running back. I had always thought men who play football on a collegiate or professional level were marvels, larger than life, super heroes. Through my letters I started to get a different perspective.

In this volume are my favorite responses to date. You will see the hand written responses to my questions on one page. On the following page you will find the transcription of the letter (some are a little difficult to read) and a bit of biographical information. Dozens of players, coaches, scouts, College and Pro Football Hall of Famers responded and told me some stories that really fascinated me. I hope reading my letters brings you a fraction of the excitement and anticipation that I got as I peeled open the envelopes that contained them.

Kindest Regards,

Craig.

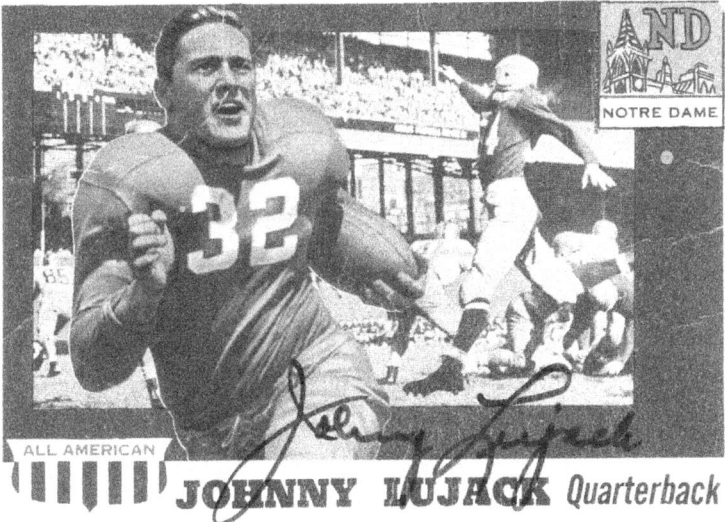

JOHNNY LUJACK *Quarterback*

A Very Brief History of Football

1869 - Rutgers and Princeton played the first documented football game.

1876 - The first rules of football were written at the Massasoit convention.

1892 - William "Pudge" Heffelfinger was paid $500 by the Allegheny Athletic Association for its game against the Pittsburgh Athletic club becoming the first professional football player.

1906 - The forward pass was legalized.

1922 - Curley Lambeau bought the Packers for $50.

1932 - In the first NFL Championship Game Chicago beat Portsmouth 9-0.

1936 - The NFL held its first collegiate draft. The Eagles chose Jay Berwanger with the first pick.

1939 - Brooklyn and Philadelphia met in the first televised NFL game.

1943 - With so many players serving in WW II, the Eagles and the Steelers combined to form the Steagles. The team was co-coached by Greasy Neale and Walt Kiesling.

1951 - The NFL Championship game was televised coast-to-coast for the first time.

1959 - Vince Lombardi replaced Ray McLean as head coach of the Green Bay Packers.

1960 - The Broncos defeated the Patriots in the American Football League's inaugural game.

1963 - The Pro Football Hall Of Fame in Canton, OH welcomed its 17 charter members.

1967 - The Packers won Super Bowl I in the Los Angeles Memorial Coliseum.

1972 - With a 17-0 record the Miami Dolphins become the first undefeated NFL team.

1974 - O.J. Simpson became the first player to rush for more than 2,000 yards.

1983 - The 1983 Draft yielded three Hall Of Fame quarterbacks: Elway, Kelly and Marino.

1989 - The Herschel Walker trade from Dallas to Minnesota involved 18 players and picks.

1998 - The Colts used the #1 pick in the draft on Peyton Manning over Ryan Leaf.

2002 - Emmitt Smith broke Walter Payton's career rushing record of 16,726 yards.

2007 - The Patriots were caught cheating in "Spy Gate" and have not won a Super Bowl since.

Bill Fischer on football after World War II:

Playing football at any college after World War II was tough because many players came back from the war to finish their education.

Some players were on the 1st or 2nd team before the war and did not make the traveling squad in 1946. We usually to the 1st, 2nd, 3rd and 4th team on our traveling squad to play the games at other schools.

The out practices were more long & hard & we scrimmaged 3 times a week. The Veterans (of the war) had to work long and hard to get their legs in shape.

Our scrimmages were tougher than some of our games and Coach Leahy was a demanding coach. It was really a great time to play college ball. I loved every minute and our friendships with our players was fantastic. Thank you for asking

Take care and God Bless!
Bill Fischer

5

Playing football at any college after World War II was tough because many players came back from the war to finish their education.

Some players were on the 1st or 2nd team before the war and did not make the traveling squad in 1946. We usually to(ok) the 1st, 2nd, 3rd and 4th team on our traveling squad to play the games at other schools.

BILL FISCHER

The practices were long and hard and we scrimmaged 3 times a week. The veterans (of the war) had to work long and hard to get their legs in shape.

Our scrimmages were tougher than some of our games and coach Leahy was a demanding coach. It was really a great time to play college ball. I loved every minute and our friendships with our players was fantastic. Thanks for asking.

Take care and God bless!

Bill Fischer

William Anton Fischer was born in Chicago, IL on March 10, 1927. He would go on to become one of the greatest linemen in the storied history of Notre Dame football. Among his long list of accomplishments was his contribution to three straight unbeaten teams from 1946 through 1948 may be the most impressive. He was named first team All-America in 1947 and 1948. In 1948 Moose took home the most prestigious award a college lineman can earn, the Outland Trophy. Fischer played in the East-West Shrine Game and the College All-Star Game following his senior year. In 1983 he was inducted into the College Football Hall Of Fame.

His hometown Chicago Cardinals selected Fischer with the 10th pick of the 1949 National Football League Draft. Moose played five seasons in the NFL for Chicago and was named to the Pro Bowl three times.

Doug Plank On The "46" Defense:

Craig,

Thanks for your letter I never thought that I would play in the NFL! It is truly taking life one step at a time. I played hard each year and every step seemed small and manageable. Playing at Ohio State and 3 Rose Rose Bowls were unforgettable. Woody Hayes taught me the value of hard work every day. Being drafted by Bears was luck. It started the opportunity to be a Chicago Bear and to be around Payton, Dhka, Singletary, Fencik and most importantly Buddy Ryan. I sold out for Ryan every game. He put me in the middle of the '46' defense and named it after my number. You never know when you are becoming a part of history. I never played in the Super Bowl but I never heard of a player or his number named for a defense.

Doug Plank #46

Craig Sievers

Craig,

Thanks for your letter. I never thought that I would play in the NFL! It is truly taking life on step at a time. I played hard each year and every step seemed small and manageable. Playing at Ohio State and 3 Rose Bowls were unforgettable. Woody Hayes taught me the value of hard work every day. Being drafted by Bears was luck. It started the opportunity to be a Chicago Bear and to be around Payton, Ditka, Singletary, Fencik and most importantly Buddy Ryan. I sold out for Ryan every game. He put me in the middle of the "46" defense and named it after my number. You never know when you are becoming a part of history. I never played in the Super Bowl but I never heard of a player or his number named for a defense.

Doug Plank #46

Douglas Walter Plank was born on March 4th, 1953 in Greensburg, Pennsylvania. Plank lasted until the twelfth round of the 1975 NFL Draft before the Bears took him with the 291st pick. He played seven full seasons at safety in Chicago. He and free safety Gary Fencik paired to create "The Hitmen."

In the "46" defense Plank, the strong safety, would play up close to the line of scrimmage to help defend against the run and

short passes over the middle. Fencik played further back and covered slot receivers and tight ends running passing routes. The corner backs were for the most part left to cover the outside receivers on their own. This defense proved very effective against short passing west coast style offenses that became popular in the 1980s.

James David "Buddy" Ryan was born in Oklahoma in 1931. From 1968 to 1995 Buddy was a coach in some capacity in the National Football League. His greatest success came with the Bears. George Halas hired Ryan in 1978 and kept him on after Mike Ditka was hired as head coach in 1982. Though they never saw eye to eye Ditka and Ryan co-existed and by 1985 Ryan's "46" defense was perfected. The 1985 Chicago Bears defense that won Super Bowl XX is still widely considered the greatest defense in modern NFL history

Ed Sprinkle on his time with the Chicago Bears:

Dear Craig

I Played Football
in High School, college
and Independence
before Joining the Bears
Bulldog Turner told me
to come try out with the
Bears and I was Fortunate
to make the Bears
I played 12 years and
was Bowl 4, Pro - All Pro
7 years.
Championship : 1946   Ed Sprinkle

Dear Craig,

I played football in high school, college and the Naval Academy before joining the Bears. Bulldog Turner told me to come try out with the Bears and I was fortunate to make the Bears. I played 12 years, made Pro Bowl 4 years, All Pro 7 Years, Championship 1946.

Ed Sprinkle

ED SPRINKLE

Edward Alexander Sprinkle was born on September 3rd, 1923 in Bradshaw, Texas. Sprinkle did indeed make George Halas' Chicago Bears in 1944. Sprinkle was a two way performer playing end on offense and defense. In the 1940's the downfield pass was just beginning to become prevalent in NFL playbooks. This helped Sprinkle on both sides of the ball. During his career Sprinkle 32 passes for 451 yards and seven touchdowns. He averaged over 14 yards per reception. However, it was when Sprinkle lined up at right defensive end that the burgeoning popularity of the forward pass allowed his talent to shine.

Ed Sprinkle is regarded as one of the first true pass rushers in NFL history. Long before Hall Of Famer Deacon Jones coined the term "sack", Sprinkle was tackling quarterbacks for losses and generally wreaking havoc behind the opposing line of scrimmage. At 6' 1" and just over 200 pounds, Sprinkle used speed, tenacity and technique to rush the quarterback. One of those techniques he employed was a violent arm rip moved that earned him the nickname "The Claw". In 1950 Collier's Magazine gave him a different nickname, "The Meanest Man In

Football". George Halas held the contention that Sprinkle was "the greatest pass rusher I've ever seen". Considering The Pro Football Hall Of Fame is located on George Halas Drive, that was quite a compliment.

Ed Sprinkle and his friend Clyde "Bulldog" Turner, another former Hardin-Simmons Cowboy, are members of the NFL 1940's All Decade Team. Turner is a member of the Pro Football Hall Of Fame, while Sprinkle still awaits the call to Canton.

Dennis Smith on the Ring Of Fame:

It was awesome being inducted!
Adding my name to all the other Great
Bronco Players that came before me.
Players that I watched & admired!
There is no better feeling than to know
that you are respected & appreciated as
one of the best players to ever put on a
Bronco uniform!

Dennis
49
Smith

It was awesome being inducted! Adding my name to all the other great Bronco players that came before me. Players that I watched & admired!

There is no better feeling than to know that you are respected & appreciated as one of the best players to ever put on a Bronco uniform!

Dennis Smith 49

Dennis Smith was born in Santa Monica, CA on February 3, 1959. Smith had a stellar career at the University of Southern California as a safety. In 1980 he was named a consensus All-American. Smith played in two Rose Bowls and was a member of the 1978 Consensus National Championship team. During his time at USC he played in the defensive backfield with future NFL Pro Bowler Joey Browner and future Pro Football Hall of Famer Ronnie Lott.

The Denver Broncos used their first round pick in 1981 to select Smith 15th overall. During the 184 games that followed Dennis proved he was "one of the best players to ever put on a Broncos uniform". He earned the reputation as one of the most intimidating hitters in the NFL as evidenced by his being named to six American Football Conference Pro Bowl squads. Smith tallied 1,152 tackles, 30 interceptions, 15 sacks, and recovered 17 fumbles. He also managed to score a touchdown. Dennis started in 170 regular season games and three Super Bowls with the Broncos. He was named to the Denver Broncos 50th Anniversary Team in 2009.

In 2001 Dennis Smith and fellow six time AFC Pro Bowler and defensive stalwart Karl Mecklenburg were inducted into the Ring of Fame at "new" Mile High Stadium.

George Blanda on his career highlight:

Just in 26 Seasons & Still able to Contribute to my team at age 48.

GB

Lasting 26 seasons & still able to contribute to my team at age 48.

GB

A 22 year old George Frederick Blanda was drafted by the Chicago Bears in the 12th round of the 1949 National Football League draft out of the University of Kentucky. A month shy of his 49th birthday, Blanda played his final game with the American Football League's Oakland Raiders. He participated in 340 professional football games over the span of those 26 seasons.

As the NFL was really taking hold as a mainstream national sport in America, George Blanda was languishing as a frustrated backup quarterback for the Bears. Legendary coach, George "Papa Bear" Halas, waited five seasons to name Blanda as first string quarterback. Soon after, an injury sidelined him for the 1954 season. From 1955 through 1959 Halas saw Blanda as solely a placekicker. Fed up, Blanda retired from the NFL after the 1959 season.

The AFL debuted in 1960 and with it the opportunity George Blanda had been seeking. The Houston Oilers signed him and named him their starting signal caller. Blanda did not disappoint. He quarterbacked the Oilers to the first two AFL Championships and took home the league's Most Valuable Player Award for the 1961 campaign. In 1962, Blanda threw a record tying seven touchdowns in a single game. The Oilers decided George Blanda was finished after the 1966 season in which they only won three games.

The Oakland Raiders thought otherwise and signed the 40 year old Blanda for the 1967 season. Finally content with being a backup quarterback and placekicker, he contributed to the AFL Championship Raiders his first season with the team. He played nine seasons in Oakland before retiring again in 1975.

The career records that George Blanda held at the time of his retirement are too numerous to list. His career was summed up by being elected to the Pro Football Hall Of Fame in the class of 1981.

Gene Hubka on the changes in the game:

FOOTBALL
(60 TO 70 YEARS AGO)

— FEWER PASSES (8 To 10 PER GAME)
— EVERYONE HAD TO PLAY 'BOTH WAYS' (OFF. + DEF.)
— QB CALLED THE PLAYS ON THE FIELD
 (TODAY PLAYS ARE CALLED FROM THE BENCH)
— WHISTLE WAS BLOWN, BY THE OFF, WHEN THE PLAYER
 HIT THE GROUND, OR WHEN THE FOWARD MOTION
 WAS STOPPED AND NOT AS TODAY 'GANG PUSHING'
— VERY FEW 'FAKE INJURIES' TODAY A PLAYER
 IS 'CARRIED OFF THE FIELD' THEN COMES
 BACK TO PLAY TWO PLAYS LATER.

Gene Hubka

Football
(60 to 70 years ago)
-Fewer passes (8 to 10 per game)
-Everyone had to play "both ways" (off. & def.)
-QB called the plays on the field (today plays are called from the bench)
-Whistle was blown by the off(icial) when the player hit the ground or when the forward motion was stopped and not as today, gang pushing.
-Very few "Fake Injuries". Today a player is carried off the field then comes back to play two plays later.
Gene Hubka

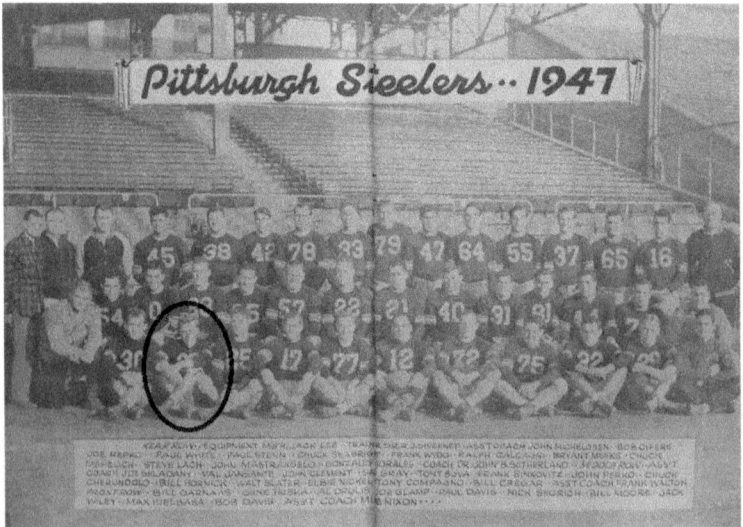

Eugene Lewis Hubka was born in Perth Amboy, New Jersey on May 18, 1924. He originally attended Temple University in

1942 and was named Honorable Mention All-America at quarterback. Hubka was sent to Bucknell University for the officer program after enlisting in the Marines during World War II. During that era Bucknell was a major national football program having won the inaugural Orange Bowl in 1935. Hubka was a versatile performer for the Bison as he played safety, punter, quarterback and halfback. His record of 140 total punt return yards in one game is still a school record. For his accomplishments on the gridiron Hubka was inducted into the Bucknell University Athletics Hall Of Fame in 1987. He was a member of the Pittsburgh Steelers during the 1946 and 1947 season.

Jimmy Orr on catching touchdown passes:

Craig,

Too many good memories playing with the Baltimore Colts. Anytime you catch a TD pass is great.

Against the Eagles in Baltimore I had a small shoulder separation. They took me to the hospital for X rays. I returned to the game and with 4 minutes left Unitas threw me a TD pass in "Orrsville" (End Zone name for me).

Jimmy Orr

Craig,

Too many good memories playing with the Baltimore Colts. Anytime you catch a TD pass is great. Against the Eagles in Baltimore I had a small shoulder separation. They took me to the hospital for X rays. I returned to the game and with 4 minutes left Unitas threw me a TD pass in "Orrsville" (end zone named for me).

Jimmy Orr

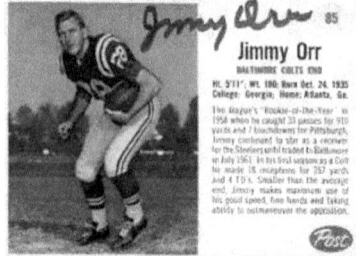

James Edward Orr Jr. was born in Seneca, NC on October 4, 1935. As a youngster Jimmy focused on basketball and baseball. Orr did not try out for the football team until his junior year of high school. Not only did he make the team, he became the starting quarterback. Although he only played two seasons and his school employed an offense that rarely had him throwing the football, Orr attracted the attention of some major college programs. Jimmy Orr Sr. urged his son to attend near-by Clemson University. The younger Orr accepted a football scholarship to play for the Tigers on the condition that he could play basketball also. The Clemson football coaches took basketball off the table so Orr transferred to a school that emphasized basketball, Wake Forest University. However, his time with the Demon Deacons was short because the basketball coaches did not see a place for him on the varsity team. Deflated, Orr transferred a third time. He attended the University Of Georgia and joined the team as a walk-on. While he had hoped to continue playing quarterback, Orr was moved to halfback and end to better utilize his soft hands as a pass catcher. He led the South Eastern Conference in receiving in 1955 and 1957.

Despite his success on the field, NFL teams were concerned about his measurables. Orr did not have blazing speed and at 5' 11" and 185 pounds his durability was in doubt. In the 1957 NFL Draft the Los Angeles Rams finally picked Orr with pick 291 intending to convert him to cornerback. However, in a preseason game against Pittsburgh Orr caught a 75 yard touchdown pass and the eye of the Steelers coaches. The Steelers orchestrated a trade and were immediately rewarded as Orr was named Rookie Of The Year. Inexplicably, Pittsburgh traded Orr to Baltimore before the 1961 season. Orr would play ten seasons with the Colts catching over 300 passes, 50 for touchdowns.

Ed Beard on money, special teams and being happy:

To Graig,

When I played and coached in the NFL all the players would have told you "I would have played for nothing because it was such a big deal Playing in the NFL." Money has taken over now and it's sad to see the NFL become what it has become.

I was Def. and Spec. Teams Capt. for five of my eight years. I was the first Special Teams Capt in the NFL. Teams finally started to learn games could be won and last with Special Teams. I was the 1st Special Team player to win the Len Eshmont Award for 49ers (Big Thrill). What I hear often "Ed you were born forty years too soon." I say no with the memories of all the great Green Bay teams - Johnny U - and all the teams and players - I wouldn't trade it for all the money in the world.

I'm happy

Ed Beard

To Craig,

When I played and coached in the NFL all the players would have told you "I would have played for nothing because it was such a big deal playing in the NFL!" Money has taken over now and it's sad to see the NFL become what it has become.

I was Def(ense) and spec(ial) teams capt(ain) for five of my eight years. I was the first special teams capt. in the NFL. Teams finally started to learn games could be won and lost with special teams. I was the 1st special team player to win the Len Eshmont Award for 49ers (Big Thrill). What I hear often "Ed you were born forty years too soon." I say <u>no</u> with the memories of all the great Green Bay teams- Johnny U- and all the teams and players. I wouldn't trade it for all the money in the world.

I'm happy

Ed Beard

Edward Leroy Beard was born in Chesapeake, VA on December 9th, 1939. At 6'1" and over 220 pounds Beard played linebacker at the University Of Tennessee. In 1964 Beard was drafted by both bay teams in California. The Oakland Raiders chose him in the 20th round of the American Football League Draft. In the National Football League Draft the San Francisco 49ers tabbed Beard in the 14th round. Beard chose the Niners and went on to play eight seasons. After injuries robbed Beard of his athleticism, he retired and went on to be an assistant coach for San Francisco, New Orleans and Detroit.

The Len Eshmont Award is given to the 49er who best exemplifies inspirational and courageous play. Len Eshmont was drafted out of Fordham University in the 5th round of the 1941 by the New York Giants. He played for the San Francisco 49ers from the inaugural 1946 season through 1949. In 1946 Eshmont scored the first touchdown in Niners history.

Larry Kaminski on his thrills with the Broncos:

CRAIG —
ALL OF MY YEARS AS A
PLAYER PROVIDED GREAT
CHALLENGES & GREAT MEMORIES.
THE BEST WAS STARTING MY
ROOKIE YEAR & GETTING INTRODUCED.
ALSO MEMORABLE... BEATING THE
RAIDERS —

ENJOY THE ENCLOSED.

Larry Kaminski
Broncos
66-73
#59

Craig-
All of my years as a player provided great challenges & great memories. The best was starting my rookie year & getting introduced. Also memorable...beating the raiders-
Enjoy the enclosed,*
Larry Kaminski
Broncos
66-73
#59

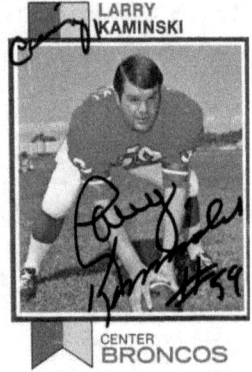

In Cleveland, OH Larry Michael Kaminski was born on January 6, 1945. After a decorated career at Cathedral Latin High School Kaminski earned an athletic scholarship to Purdue University. He played linebacker and center for the Boilermakers and was a teammate of future Pro Football Hall Of Famer Bob Griese. Kaminski started at center for three seasons and was named All Big Ten and Honorable Mention All-America in 1965. The 1966 NFL Draft consisted of twenty rounds and the AFL Draft had twelve. During all those rounds no team saw fit to choose Larry Kaminski.

Kaminski was content to take the bachelors degree he earned at Purdue and start a career in the business world when he got a call from the Denver Broncos. The Broncos wanted to give Kaminski a shot to make the team as a free agent. Larry jumped at the chance to earn a roster spot and joined the team at their training camp on the campus of the Colorado School Of Mines in Golden, CO. By the time camp broke and the team headed back to Denver, Larry Kaminski had not only made the team, he was the starting center.

From 1966 through 1973 Kaminski started 68 games and participated in 96 games in total. He was named an AFL All Star for his performance during the 1967 season. After injuries took their toll and caused Kaminski to retire he became a successful businessman in Colorado. He later moved to Washington state and owned and operated Captain Larry's Adventures, a charter fishing service.

*What he "enclosed" with his response was a two DVD set of 1960s Broncos game footage from his personal film collection. I did enjoy them.

Charlie Hennigan on his greatest season:

1961 Season
12 TDS
1746 yards/Over 20 yds av. Per Catch
Conference Champions
Averaged over 40 Points Per
game
ALL-Pro

Charlie Hennigan Oilers
60-66

1961 Season
12 TDs
1746 yards/ over 20 yds av. per catch
Conference Champions
Averaged over 40 points per game
All-Pro
Charlie Hennigan- Oilers 60-66

Charles Taylor Hennigan was born in Bienville Parish, Louisiana on March 19, 1935. Charlie attended Minden High School and was name All-North Louisiana in football and track. He accepted an athletic scholarship to run track at Louisiana State University.

Hennigan wanted to play football for coach Gaynel Tinsley's Tigers but at the time it was not permitted for him to play both sports. He transferred to Northwestern State College in Natchitoches, Louisiana. From 1954 through 1957 Hennigan starred for the Northwestern State Demons on both the track and the gridiron. He was All-Conference at half back and also played cornerback. In 1958 Hennigan graduated with a bachelor's degree in education.

Being that Northwestern State was such a small school it was not surprising that Hennigan was passed over in the 1958 NFL Draft. Charlie went to Canada to further his football career and landed a tryout with the three time Grey Cup winner Edmonton Eskimos. After only a month Hennigan returned to the states after the Eskimos coach Sam Lyle said he was too dumb to learn the offense. He returned to Northwestern State and earned his master's degree.

Hennigan got a job teaching at Jonesboro-Hodge High School in Jonesboro, Louisiana. While he was there he continued to stay in shape by working out with former All-Pro NFL receiver Dub Jones. Jones instructed Hennigan on some of the nuances of route running and how to get open.

After hearing about a new professional football league Hennigan and his friend Charlie Tolar decided to try out. They drove (and hitch hiked) to Houston and both made the Oilers. Hennigan caught the first touchdown in Oilers history on a 43 yard pass from George Blanda. His 1746 yards was a pro record until 1985 and still ranks fourth all-time. Hennigan was an All Pro three times and named to five Pro Bowl squads.

Elois Grooms on tough offensive linemen:

Craig the hardest thing for me to do would be to pick out the toughest lineman that I played against. These guys usually were bigger and probably out weighed me on average about 75 pounds. I played against a lot of linemen that are now in Canton, Ohio as a member of the NFL HALL of FAME and they deserve to be. The list of players such as 'ANTHONY MUNOZ', 'JACKIE SLATER', 'JOHN HANNAH', 'Gene upshaw', 'Art shell', 'Dan Dierdorf', are just a few of a long line of greats. There is one that perhaps gave me more trouble than the 'Hall of fame' guys and that was 'WARREN Bryant'. ATLANTA FALCON first round pick out of UNIVERSITY of KENTUCK. He was tall 6'7" and had the longest arms of any of my opponents. The long arms made it very difficult to get to his body and that created a tough day on the football field. Warren has received the vote from me as my toughest player or better offensive lineman. He probably will never be in the 'HALL of FAME' but he always was a tough opponent SAINTS Vs. FALCONS.

Elois Grooms
78

Craig Sievers

Craig the hardest thing for me to do would be to pick out the toughest linemen that I played against. These guys were bigger and probably outweighed me on average about 75 pounds. I played against a lot of linemen that are now in Canton, Ohio as a member of the NFL Hall Of Fame and they deserve to be. The list of players such as 'Anthony Munoz', 'Jackie Slater', 'John Hannah', 'Gene Upshaw', 'Art Shell', 'Dan Dierdorf', are just a few of the long line of greats. There is one that perhaps gave me more trouble than the 'Hall Of Fame' guys and that was 'Warren Bryant', Atlanta Falcons first round pick out of University Of Kentucky. He was tall 6' 7" and had the longest arms of any of my opponents. The long arms made it very difficult to get to his body and that created a tough day on the football field. Warren has received the vote from me as my toughest player or better offensive linemen. He probably will never be in the Hall Of Fame but he always was a tough opponent Saints vs. Falcons.

Elois Grooms #78

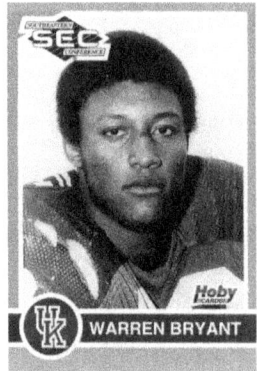

Tompkinsville, KY welcomed Elois T. Grooms on May 20, 1953. Grooms opted to matriculate at Tennessee Tech University because the coaching staff would allow him to play defense. At 6' 4" and just over 200 pounds, other interested colleges had wanted to convert him to tight end. Grooms played defensive line for the Golden Eagles and filled out to a solid 250 pounds. The New Orleans Saints selected Grooms in the third round of the 1975 NFL Draft. After his first season in New Orleans, he returned to Cookeville and completed his degree at Tennessee Tech. For five consecutive seasons with the Saints, Grooms started every game. He started 79 games over his seven seasons with the Saints. Grooms spent four seasons with the St. Louis Cardinals and one final season with the Philadelphia Eagles. Elois and his wife Judy (they met her freshman year) were co-recipients of the Outstanding Alumni Award for Education at Tennessee Tech in 2013.

Warren Bryant (1955-) was a star tackle at the University Of Kentucky and was the sixth overall pick in the 1977 NFL Draft. He played eight seasons in Atlanta starting 93 of the 99 games in which he played. Bryant was Kentucky's 2005 honoree for the SEC Football Legends.

Clarence "Ace" Parker On baseball vs. football:

ENJoyed BASEbALL
The most - iT WAS FuN
FooTBALL was work.
I didNT pLAy BASebALL
As good As FooTBALL -

"Ace"

Enjoyed baseball the most- it was fun. Football was work. I didn't play baseball as good as football.

"Ace"

"ACE" PARKER   *Quarterback*

Clarence "Ace" Parker was born May 17th, 1912 in Portsmouth, Virginia. Ace starred in baseball, basketball and football at Duke University. From 1934 through 1936, Parker led Duke in rushing, passing, punting and kick returns. His 105 yard kick return is still a school record. For his exploits on the gridiron, Parker was named All-America in both '35 and '36 and finished sixth in the Heisman voting in 1936. He was inducted into the College Football Hall Of Fame in 1955.

Baseball was still the glamour sport in America in the 1930's. Parker planned on leaving football behind for the diamond and signed with Connie Mack's Philadelphia Athletics. In 1937 Ace played 38 games at shortstop for the A's. In 94 times at bat Parker managed only 11 hits for a .117 batting average. After his less than stellar rookie season with the A's Parker was given permission to give football a try with the NFL team that had drafted him in 1937, the Brooklyn Dodgers.

While he only expected to play one season with Brooklyn, Parker became a multi sport phenomenon. He was Bo Jackson 50 years before Bo Jackson. In 1938 and 1940 Parker was named NFL All Pro. He was the National Football League Most Valuable Player in 1940. With all his success on the football field Parker played only one more season for the A's before hanging up his glove and cap for good after the 1938 season. In 1942 through 1945 Parker served in the Navy during World War

II. Parker served honorably and was discharged in time for the 1945 football season.

He played one season with the short lived Boston Yanks of the NFL and one for the New York Yankees of All American Football Conference. Parker led coach Ray Flaherty's club to a playoff win before falling to the mighty Cleveland Browns in the 1946 AAFC Championship. He was inducted into the Pro Football Hall Of Fame in 1972. Clarence Parker passed away on November 6th, 2013 at 101 years old.

Gil Brandt on Tex Schramm:

NATIONAL FOOTBALL LEAGUE

16 January 2013

Dear Craig,

Tex and I began working together when he was with the Los Angeles Rams. Pete Rozelle ran the Rams in the late 1950's before he moved onto become one of the greatest commissioners in sports history.

Before the 1960 season, Clint Murchison was awarded a franchise in Dallas by the NFL and both Tex and I made the move. Coach Landry was hired away from the NY Giants, where he was their defensive coordinator after a stellar career as a defensive back.

We all lived near each other in Dallas and shared a common bond for football and growing the sport in this area. The early days were a little difficult, but we survived and fought our way to the top eventually.

Thanks for your interest in the NFL and the Dallas Cowboys.

Sincerely,

Gil Brandt

Tommy Mason on being the 1ˢᵗ Minnesota Viking:

Hi Craig

Thanks for the very nice note....actually, at that time, I was not overly aware of being the "first" Viking....when you are a member of the "team" of any sport or kind, you are aware that your fate or how well you do, is dependent upon every single other person in addition to yourself.....and although you do the best job you can, your success is dependent upon all of the other team members.

In my particular case, I was, and still am, very proud of my Viking years. In those first Viking years I was fortunate to be playing behind Hugh McElhenny, one of the all time greats in the league. It didn't dawn on me at the time, but he was probably more aware of what I was going to go through than I was. The first 3 years I was his back up on offense and ran back punts and kick offs, so that gave me a chance to learn from one of the league's all time greats in addition to playing special teams on punts and kick offs at the same time. I played in the Pro Bowl in my second, third and fourth years; and was all pro my third year.

As far as being the first Viking in their history, I was, and I am, extremely proud of that. Later in the year, Joe Thomas, the Viking coach that was in charge of the draft, told me, that I would have been the first choice on about half of the other teams in the league, but that situation is controlled by the strength and "needs" of the other positions on a particular team. I remember Joe telling me that I would have been the first choice on about 60 % of the other teams in the league.

That year, 1961, was also the first year in the history of the American Football league and I was also one of two first round choices in the history of the Boston Patriots. Along with me, the other Patriot choice was Ken Rice of Auburn. That was before the leagues came together and it was flattering to be drafted #1 in that league also. If fact, that was the first round, of the first year, of the American Football League, which, as you are aware, is now the American conference of the NFL!

At any rate Craig, those are some of the factors that existed when I was 20 years old and yesterday, July 8, was my 71ˢᵗ birthday.....only a quick 50 years ago...Thanks for you interest and giving me a excuse to brush away some cobwebs from my brain!

They say "timing" is everything!!! YOU THINK???

Best Wishes!

Tommy Mason

Forrest Behm on perseverance:

When I was five years old I started a fire in a prairie near my home in Lincoln. I was bedridden for a long time. My father refused to allow the doctors to amputate one leg. In my day we had very little skill in handling serious burns. I have a scar on my entire right leg. I had to learn all over—how to run and to throw. I was bedridden for a long time. I had to learn how to walk again. My father taught me to walk and how to run—throw a ball and play football. Don't ever give up. You can learn over it next.

Never give up—
Warm regards
and good luck—

Forrest Behm

When I was five years old I started a fire in a prairie near my home in Lincoln. I was bed ridden for a long time. My father refused to allow the doctors to amputate one leg. In my day we had very little skill in handling serious burns. I have a scar on my entire right leg. I had to learn all over how to run and to throw. I was bedridden for a long time. I had to learn how to walk again. My father taught me to walk and how to run, throw a ball and play football. <u>Don't ever give up</u>. You can learn over if need be.

Never give up-
Warm regards and good luck-
Forrest Behm

Forrest Edwin Behm was born in Lincoln, NE on July 31, 1919. Despite the diligence of his parents, Behm would not regain full mobility in his leg until his senior year of high school. Although he was 6'4", by far the tallest player, Behm was told he would not make the varsity basketball team at Lincoln High due to lingering issues from his injury. He still had a desire to compete athletically so he went out for the football team. Considering he had never played an organized game before it was no surprise that Behm played sparingly during his one season of prep football.

Forrest stayed in town and attended the University Of Nebraska. By the time he attempted to try out as a walk-on with the Cornhuskers, Behm had packed 200 pounds onto his frame.

Were he to make the team he would immediately be one of the biggest players. Even in the 1930's football was a big man's game and Behm's size offset his lack of experience on the gridiron. Due to the depression the Huskers athletic department did not have the funds available to buy size 15 cleats for Behm. He had to purchase his own cleats before he was allowed to make the squad.

Two short years later Forrest Behm had added another 25 pounds and become a mammoth yet nimble offensive and defensive tackle for the 7th ranked Nebraska Cornhuskers. After an 8-1 record during the 1940 season the Huskers earned an invite to their first bowl game in program history. Though they fell to Stanford in the 1941 Rose Bowl, Nebraska had established itself as a football power. Behm was named First Team All-America for the 1940 season.

Dale Dodrill on playing for the Pittsburgh Steelers:

Nine years with the same team "Pittsburgh Steelers" A great
owner - Art Rooney - and great fans!

No face masks
Goal post were on the goal line.
33 players to a team
You had to hold a ball carrier down and in your
grasp until the whistle blew or he could get
up and continue running.
Water buckets on the field had oatmeal in it so
players wouldn't drink the water.

Craig - Wishing you a Blessed and Joyful
Holiday Season!

Best regards,
Dale Dodrill

Craig Sievers

Nine years with the same team "Pittsburgh Steelers". A great owner- Art Rooney- and great fans!

No face masks

Goal posts were on the goal line

33 players to a team

You had to hold a ball carrier down and in your grasp until the whistle blew or he could get up and continue running.

Water buckets on the field had oatmeal in it so players wouldn't drink the water.

Craig- wishing you a blessed and joyful holiday season!

Best regards,

Dale Dodrill

Dale Dodrill was born in Stockton, KS on February 7, 1926. He went to high school in Loveland, CO. While at Loveland High Dodrill helped lead the Indians to a state championship in 1942. After graduation he joined the Army. Dodrill served honorably in Europe during World War II and was ready to play football immediately upon returning stateside. Denver University and University of Colorado at Boulder would not let the war vet play his freshman year. Colorado State University agreed to add the 6'1" 220 pound linebacker to the active roster immediately if he was good enough to make the team. Dodrill made the varsity squad as a freshman and helped contribute to the greatest era in CSU football history. Dodrill teamed with future NFL All-Pro Thurman "Fum" McGraw and future Pro Football Hall Of Famer Jack Christiansen to lead the Rams to the 1949 Raisin Bowl.

The Pittsburgh Steelers chose Dodrill with pick 57 in the 1951 NFL Draft, two picks ahead of his college teammate Christiansen. In nine seasons in the Steel City Dodrill was named to four Pro Bowls and was named a first team All-Pro in 1954. Dodrill was named to the Pittsburgh Steelers Legends team during the team's 75th anniversary celebration in 2007. After his career as a player ended Dodrill returned to Colorado to help coach the newly formed Denver Broncos in 1960.

Bill Renna on choosing baseball over football:

Dear Craig:

I always wanted to be a baseball player. I played baseball when I was very young, & always loved the game.

I didn't play football until my senior year in high school. I went to U.S.F. after I graduated — & played football & baseball @ U.S.F. I went into the Marine Corps after a year @ U.S.F and then went to Menlo Jr. College when I was discharged. From Menlo I went to Santa Clara Univ. in spring of '47. I played football and baseball @ S.C.U.

I was drafted by the L.A. Dons in the American Football league — and the L.A. Rams in the N.F.L. The Dons offered me $7000.00 — but I went with the N.Y. Yankees for $6000.00

Regards,
Bill Renna

> *Dear Craig,*
>
> *I always wanted to be a baseball player. I played baseball when I was very young & always loved the game.*
>
> *I didn't play football until my senior year in high school. I went to U.S.F. after I graduated & played football & baseball at U.S.F. I went into the Marine Corps after a year at U.S.F. and then went to Menlo Jr. College when I was discharged. From Menlo I went to Santa Clara Uni. in the spring of '47. I played football and baseball at S.C.U.*
>
> *I was drafted by the L.A. Dons in the American Football League and the L.A. Rams in the NFL. The Dons offered me $7000.00, but I went with the N.Y. Yankees for $6000.00.*
>
> *Regards, Bill Renna*

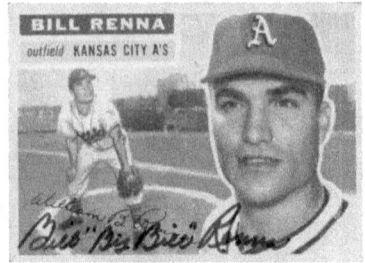

William Beneditto Renna was born in Hanford, CA on October 14th, 1924. "Big Bill" stood 6'3" weighed nearly 220 pounds and played fullback for the Santa Clara University Broncos during the 1947 and 1948 seasons. From 1896 through 1952 Santa Clara University played some of the best regional and national competition in college football. The Broncos played home games at Kezar Stadium where the AAFC and NFL's San Francisco 49ers called home from 1946 until 1970.

Santa Clara was preparing to take on the University Of Southern California Trojans during Renna's senior season and both the team's centers were injured. Coach Len Casanova asked the his rugged fullback to try a few snaps at center. After snapping three times to his coach Renna was inserted as the starting center against USC. Pro teams took notice of Big Bill's versatility. Renna was drafted by the Los Angeles Rams with pick 117 of the 1949 NFL Draft. The Chicago Bears took University Of Kentucky quarterback George Blanda with pick 119.

Bill Renna did indeed accept the New York Yankees offer and made his Major League debut on April 14th, 1953. Renna played outfield and pinch hitter for six seasons with the Yankees, Athletics and Red Sox.

Gary Glick on being the #1 pick in the draft:

Hi Craig —

I survived a lot of Needling + cheap shots early in the season — my 1st game I lost 4 teeth by an elbow shot — Paul Brown called me Bonus Baby during the game & I missed the last 4 games as a rookie due to a Broken Jaw Broken cheek bone & Broken nose + 17 stitches — I was hit by a Team mate in a pile up — Jack Butler — one of Pitts great DB's — We didn't have masks as they do now — I'll send along a couple items from the past — I still get fan mail — suprising, isn't it?

Good Luck with your project

Gary Glick

Hi Craig-

I survived a lot of heckling & cheap shots early in the season. My 1ˢᵗ game I lost 4 teeth by an elbow shot. Paul Brown called me Bonus Baby during the game & I missed the last 4 games as a rookie due to a broken jaw, broken cheek bone, broken nose & 17 stitches. I was hit by a team mate in a pile up, Jack Butler, one of Pitt's great DB's. We

GARY GLICK
HALFBACK   PITTSBURGH STEELERS

didn't have masks as they do now. I'll send along a couple of items from the past. I still get fan mail, surprising isn't it?

Good luck with your project,
Gary Glick

Grant, NE welcomed Gary Gaylen Glick on May 14th, 1930. When he graduated Cache La Poudre High School in Laporte, CO he weighed a little over 160 pounds. After serving four years in the United States Navy Glick came home a chiseled 195. Though he was highly regarded by many top football schools he stayed home and went on to star at Colorado A&M (State) University. On offense he played running back, quarterback and receiver and he twice lead the team in rushing and was the Rams leading passer in 1954. When the Rams took the field on defense Glick played safety, linebacker and end setting a career record with 14 interceptions. He even capably handled the place kicking duties. In 1992 Glick was voted as a member of the Colorado State All Century Team as a running back. Over 10,000 ballots were collected.

Glick was the number one overall pick in the 1956 NFL Draft by the Pittsburgh Steelers. He played for the Pittsburgh Steelers, Washington Redskins, Baltimore Colts and San Diego Chargers. During his one season with the Chargers he was a member of the 1963 AFL Champions. Gary Glick was inducted into the Colorado Sports Hall Of Fame in 1992.

Billy Shaw on his Buffalo Bills career:

CRAIG,

Thanks for your Letter And Request. So MANY Great things happened for me As A Bill - Two AFL titles, Captain of Team 8 yr's, 8 All-Star Games, 5 times All AFL, All Time AFL Team, HoF IN 1999 — Great Memories.

CRAIG, I Can't forget the Loss to KC IN the 1966 AFL Championship Game. The Winner went to Super Bowl #1. We Lost.

Over All My time in Buffalo was A Life Changing Experience - Would Not Change A thing —

Billy

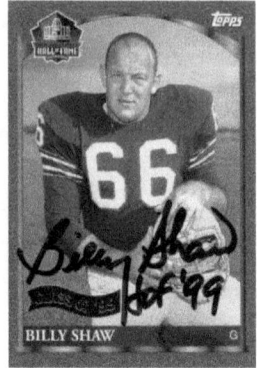

Craig,

Thanks for your letter and request. So many great things happened for me as a Bill- two AFL titles, captain of team 8 yr's, 8 All Star games, 5 times All AFL, All Time AFL Team, HOF in 1999- great memories.

Craig, I can't forget the loss to KC in the 1966 AFL Championship Game. The winner went to Super Bowl #1. We lost.

Overall my time in Buffalo was a life changing experience. Would not change a thing.

Billy

On December 15, 1938 Vicksburg, MS welcomed the arrival of William Lewis Shaw. Billy would grow to be an excellent athlete. By the time he was a senior in high school he weighed in at close to 200 pounds and played tackle on offense and defense. Shaw had originally intended to go to a college in Mississippi to stay closer to home. While choosing between Mississippi State or Ole Miss, Shaw had a surprise encounter that would change his mind. Former "Mississippi Mr. Football" and fellow Vicksburg native George Morris visited the Shaw home around dinner time. Morris had been an All American for Georgia Tech in 1952 and accompanying him that evening was Tech's head coach Bobby Dodd. By the end of supper with Morris and Dodd, Shaw was ready to travel the 500 miles to attend school in Atlanta.

Billy Shaw went on to be a force on offense and defense for the Yellow Jackets and was named All SEC Third Team his junior season and All SEC First Team his senior season. In 1961 he was chosen by the Buffalo Bills in the second round of the AFL Draft and by The Dallas Cowboys in round 14 of the NFL Draft. The Cowboys intended to convert Shaw to linebacker while the Bills envisioned him as an offensive guard. Shaw decided to sign with the Bills. It turned out to be a fortuitous decision for both Billy Shaw and the Buffalo Bills. For his nine stellar seasons as a pulling guard Shaw earned a bust in Canton. He is the only member of the Pro Football Hall Of Fame to play his entire career in the American Football League.

Al Wistert on having his number retired, twice:

Dear Craig Seevers –

Yes, my number "11" was retired
to honor my two brothers & me. My
number #70 was the first number ever
retired for anyone by the Phila. Eagles.
I played for 9 yrs with the Eagles
8 years chosen All-Pro. Am still not in
the NFL Hall of Fame – but should be.

Regards
Al "ox" Wistert

Craig Sievers

Dear Craig Sievers-

Yes, my number "11" was retired to honor my two brothers & me. My number #70 was the first number ever retired for anyone by the Phila. Eagles. I played 9 yrs with the Eagles. 8 years chosen All-Pro. I'm still not in the NFL Hall of Fame- but should be.

Regards,

Al "Ox" Wistert

Albert Alexander Wistert was not yet known as "Ox" when he was born in Chicago on December 28th, 1920. He and his three brothers all played tackle at the University Of Michigan and all wore jersey number 11. Before his first game with the Wolverines in 1940 Wistert had never played an organized game of football. By the time he left the college football gridiron he had been named All American and was the team Most Valuable Player in 1942. Francis, Alvin and Albert were inducted together into the University Of Michigan Hall Of Honor in 1981.

"Ox" as drafted by the Philadelphia Eagles in the fifth round of the 1943 NFL draft. For the 1943 season, due to World War II, the Eagles merged with the Pittsburgh Steelers to form the Steagles. Wistert was a member of NFL Championship teams in Philadelphia in 1948 and 1949. Both championship victories were by shut out.

As a member of the 1940's NFL All Decade Team, an All Pro eight times and Eagles team captain for five seasons, "Ox" Wistert probably "should be" in the Pro Football Hall Of Fame.

76

CHAMPIONSHIPS

All-Time Super Bowl Results

I	Green Bay 35, Kansas City 10	X	Pittsburgh 21, Dallas 17
II	Green Bay 33, Oakland 14	XI	Oakland 32, Minnesota 14
III	NY Jets 16, Baltimore Colts 7	XII	Dallas 27, Denver 10
IV	Kansas City 23, Minnesota 7	XIII	Pittsburgh 35, Dallas 31
V	BAL Colts 16, Dallas 13	XIV	Pittsburgh 31, Los Angeles 19
VI	Dallas 24, Miami 3	XV	Oakland 27, Philadelphia 10
VII	Miami 14, Washington 7	XVI	San Francisco 26, Cincinnati 21
VIII	Miami 24, Minnesota 7	XVII	Washington 27, Miami 17
IX	Pittsburgh 16, Minnesota 6	XVIII	Los Angeles 38, Washington 9

XIX	San Francisco 38, Miami 16		XXIX	San Francisco 49, San Diego 26
XX	Chicago 46, New England 10		XXX	Dallas 27, Pittsburgh 17
XXI	NY Giants 39, Denver 20		XXXI	Green Bay 35, New England 21
XXII	Washington 42, Denver 10		XXXII	Denver 31, Green Bay 24
XXIII	San Francisco 20, Cincinnati 16		XXXIII	Denver 34, Atlanta 19
XXIV	San Francisco 55, Denver 10		XXXIV	St. Louis 23, Tennessee 16
XXV	NY Giants 20, Buffalo 19		XXXV	BAL Ravens 34, NY Giants 7
XXVI	Washington 37, Buffalo 24		XXXVI	New England 20, St. Louis 17
XXVII	Dallas 52, Buffalo 17		XXXVII	Tampa Bay 48, Oakland 21
XXVIII	Dallas 30, Buffalo 13		XXXVIII	New England 32, Carolina 29

XXXIX	New England 24, Philadelphia 21	**XLIV**	New Orleans 31, Indianapolis 17
XL	Pittsburgh 21, Seattle 10	**XLV**	Green Bay 31, Pittsburgh 25
XLI	Indianapolis 29, Chicago 17	**XLVI**	NY Giants 21, New England 17
XLII	NY Giants 17, New England 14	**XLVII**	BAL Ravens 34, San Francisco 31
XLIII	Pittsburgh 27, Arizona 23	**XLVIII**	STL Seahawks 43, Denver Broncos 8

Coach Weeb Ewbank on Joe Namath's "Guarantee":

Our motto for the game was — Maintain your POISE and EXECUTE flawlessly! The 2 word P.+E. are on our Championship ring!

Joe said he replied to a question - WhoWillWin?

was how he felt - Jets!!! Also, it was my fault because the whole team felt that way because of our preparations for the game!

Weeb Ewbank

<u>Our motto</u> for the game was-maintain you <u>Poise</u> and <u>Execute</u> flawlessly! The 2 words P.&E. are on our Championship ring!

Joe said he replied to a question-<u>Who will win?</u>

Was how he felt- Jets!!! Also, it was my fault because the whole team felt that way because of our preparations for the game!

Weeb Ewbank

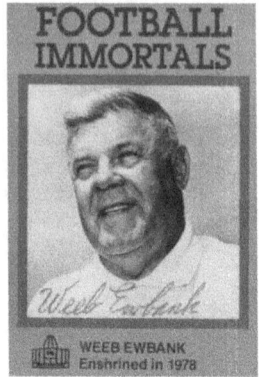

FOOTBALL IMMORTALS

WEEB EWBANK
Enshrined in 1978

Wilbur Charles Ewbank was born in Richmond, IN on May 6, 1907. Ewbank was a multi-sport athlete in high school lettering in baseball, basketball and football. At Miami University Of Ohio he continued to play all three sports including quarterbacking the Red Hawks to the Ohio Athletic Conference title his senior season of 1927.

From 1928 through 1943 Ewbank coached high school football. His combined record as a prep coach at Van Wert High and McGuffey High was 71-21. In 1936 his McGuffey team went undefeated while not allowing any opposing team to score a single point all season.

In 1943 Ewbank joined the United States Navy. He was assigned to the Naval Station Great Lakes where Paul Brown was the coach of the base football team. Brown was no stranger to Ewbank, they were classmates and teammates at Miami. Ewbank assisted Brown, who was by then the head coach at Ohio State, on the football team and was the head coach of the basketball squad. After World War II Ewbank coached two seasons at Washington University in St. Louis leading the Bears to a 14-4 record.

In 1949 he took the opportunity to assist Paul Brown again, this time with the Cleveland Browns. The Browns won championships in 1949 and 1950. He spent four seasons in Cleveland before taking the head coaching position with the Baltimore Colts. After a couple tough seasons of building up the roster, Ewbank led the Colts to back-to-back NFL Championships in 1958 and 1959. A decade later Ewbank would guide the New York Jets to a Super Bowl III victory. He is the only coach to win a championship with an AFL and an NFL team. Weeb Ewbank was named to the Pro Football Hall Of Fame in the class of 1978.

Lou Sossamon on the 1946 AAFC Championship:

My highlight was playing
Cleveland Browns for championships and
being paid $800 for the game. Browns
were paid $1000 for winning.

Regards,
Lou Sossamon

My highlight was playing Cleveland Browns for Championship being paid $800 for the game. Browns were paid $1000 for winning.

Regards, Lou Sossamon

LOU SOSSAMON

Lou Cody Sossamon was born on June 2, 1921 in Gaffney, South Carolina. He stayed in state for his college career and played for the South Carolina Gamecocks. Sossamon was a Second Team All-American after the 1942 campaign. He was the first ever Gamecock to be named All-American. Twice Sossamon was named All-Southern Conference.

His playing days did not end with his graduation. The Pittsburgh Steagles chose Sossamon with the 47th pick in the NFL Draft. Before he could suit up for the Pittsburgh/Philadelphia pro team, Sossamon entered the U.S. Navy. Sossamon played football while he was stationed at Pearl Harbor. Before he was "The Man", Stan Musial was the water boy for Sossamon's Navy football team.

His service time complete, Sossamon signed to play center and linebacker with the New York Yanks of the All American Football Conference. Future Pro Football Hall Of Famers Tom Landry, Frank "Bruiser" Kinard, Clarence "Ace" Parker and Arnie Weinmeister were team mates of Sossamon's during his time in New York.

The 1946 AAFC Championship was played at Cleveland Stadium in front of more than 41,000 fans. The game was a defensive battle. The Browns offensive fire power of Otto

Graham, Dante Glue Fingers" Lavelli, Lou "The Toe" Groza and Marion Motley, had just enough to put Cleveland on top 14-9. The AAFC merged with the NFL after the 1949 season.

Dick Brubaker on The Ohio State Buckeyes:

Dear Craig:

Thank you for your interest. My experience at Ohio State was one of the most interesting and exciting times of my life. I was surrounded by great players with character and great coaches with great character as well. The fact that we were undefeated, Rose Bowl victors and National Champions was frosting on the cake.

I would not have missed it for the world.

Take good care
Dick Brubaker
OSU 1954
Go Bucks!

Craig Sievers

Dear Craig:

Thank you for your interest. My experience at Ohio State was one of the most interesting and exciting times of my life. I was surrounded by great players with character and great coaches with great character as well. The fact that we were undefeated, Rose Bowl victors and National Champions was frosting on the cake.

I would not have missed it for the world.

Take good care

Dick Brubaker

OSU 1954

Go Bucks!

Dick Brubaker took the scenic route to the Rose Bowl. He was born on January 2, 1932 in Cleveland, OH. Brubaker played his high school football for the Shaker Heights Raiders that won the 1949 Lake Erie Championship. After graduation, he enrolled and played two seasons at Ohio Wesleyan University in Delaware, OH. As a member of the Battling Bishops in 1951 Brubaker helped Wesleyan bring home the Ohio Athletic Conference championship. After two years, Brubaker sought a greater challenge and decided to transfer to Ohio State University.

Legendary coach Woody Hayes was persuaded to allow Brubaker try out as a walk on to the Buckeyes as an offensive end. Brubaker made first team halfway through the 1953 season.

Although he never received an athletic scholarship at Columbus, Brubaker was elected a team co-captain in 1954. Ohio State has been participating in football since 1890. That 1954 season the Buckeyes went 10-0 for the first time in school history. The Rose Bowl was a 20-7 victory over the University Of Southern California Trojans.

Brubaker was drafted by the Chicago Cardinals in the 15th round of the 1955 NFL Draft. He played three professional seasons interrupted by 18 months served in the Navy. After his playing days, Dick Brubaker embarked on an extremely successful career as a lawyer in Cleveland.

Matt Snell on scoring in the Super Bowl:

Scoring a T.D. in the Super Bowl
is a honor that is shared with few others.
It puts one in a group, that is very select!
One remembers it always as if it was yesterday!
A True Honor!

Matt Snell

Scoring a TD in the Super Bowl is an honor that is shared with few others. It puts one in a group that is very select! One remembers it always as if it was yesterday! A true honor!

Matt Snell

Though he would grow up in the small town of Carle Place, New York, Matt Snell was born in Garfield, Georgia in 1941. After starring as a halfback for the Carle Place Frogs, Snell attended Ohio State University. He was an extremely versatile performer for the Buckeyes. During his three seasons as a starter on the varsity squad Snell played three different positions. As a sophomore he was mainly a blocking back for future Pro Football Hall Of Famer Paul Warfield. The next season Snell switched to the other side of the line of scrimmage and played defense. He earned his place on the Ohio State Football All-Century Team for his one season at defensive end. Finally during his senior season Snell took his place at starting fullback which was the main ball carrier in Woody Hayes' offense. With his punishing running style and understanding of run and pass blocking, Matt Snell was destined to play football as a professional.

The New York Jets chose Snell with the third overall pick in the first round of the 1964 AFL Draft. The New York Giants chose Snell in the NFL Draft as well. New York's NFL team waited until the fourth round to tab the Ohio State back and offered him very little money to sign. Matt Snell chose the Jets in what would turn out to be an important signing for the still developing American Football League. At that time the NFL still had the edge in signing draft picks from the power conference colleges. The AFL was still trying to mine diamonds in the rough of the smaller schools in the country. Alabama's star quarterback would sign with the Jets in 1965.

On the field the Jets showed that the AFL could compete with the NFL as well. The Jets second offensive play in Super Bowl III was a run during which Snell knocked Baltimore's star safety Rick Volk unconscious. It was a precursor for Snell's performance that day as he would carry the ball thirty times for 121 yards. His touchdown in second quarter gave the underdog Jets a lead that they would never relinquish against the powerful Colts.

Vagas Ferguson on the 1977 National Champions:

January 11, 2013

Dear Craig;

It's not often I get asked about the '77 National Championship.

Well, for starter's Notre Dame was rated 5th in the nation at that time with one loss our match up with number 1 Texas (12-0) was slated as an eventual major loss.

Texas at that time had the following:

Rated number one in the country
Earl Campbell – Heisman Trophy winner that year
Outland Trophy winner – Best defensive player
Best field goal/extra point kicker in the country
Two wide receivers that were world class sprinters
And the best offenses / defenses in the country

So, you see what we were up against. But, I can't recall while we were preparing for the game that it was ever said or thought among the players that we didn't have a chance. I am not sure what the coaches were thinking. I do know it was business as usual for us. If they had any doubts they weren't apparent to us.

I think people thought that we were so out matched that as players we were probably scared of playing in such a big game with national champ consequences. And little do people know we never once thought if we defeated Texas that we would become number one. But we were excited to be in the big game, and we were there to compete especially when everybody had written us off.

The advantage we had going into the game I felt was the big game experiences. Being Notre Dame at that time was a nationally recognized program meaning every game was a big game because an opponent's season was made complete if they beat us. So, we had no problem focusing on the game itself it was basically another game that ended up with national ramifications.

The game itself was about the same basic things you practice every day carrying out your assignments.

I can't say winning the National Championship isn't special especially to see how long it's been since ND has won one. But, now that I am older and a lot of years removed from playing the game, it was a monumental feat to have won.

Thanks, for asking for my thoughts on the national championship it was nice to reminisce.

God Bless

Vagas

Tom Nowatzke on Super Bowl V:

Craig,

Thank you for writing me. This is an interesting story about Super Bowl V. We thought going into the game that we could run strong side which meant me blocking for Norm Bulaich. Three times in the first half, they stopped us inside the 20 short yardage. So we said at half time that we were going to go weak side which means I carry the ball weak side in the first short yardage play. Well, the first short yardage play was with first and ten on the four. So on second and ten I carried to the left and ran right up the tight end's block and we didn't get in. I went back to the huddle and told Earl Morell to please run it again because I screwed the play up. It wasn't exactly in those words. Lo and behold he did. It was third and two on the two and we were behind by seven. In today's ball game they would call time out and everybody and their brother would be trying to figure out what to do. But Earl just called the play, we went up and ran it, and we scored. So I keep kidding Earl, who now has some dementia problems, that I had to call the play for him. But Earl and I are good friends. It was a great time, and that's all I can say.

You didn't know that this game would go to the heights that it has and it's still going when we were playing. Tickets to the Super Bowl were $15. Now if you want to go this year, I think the minimum is $800 and the most expensive is $1,200. What a change.

Thanks for your interest.

Tom Nowatzke

Tom Nowatzke

TOM NOWATZKE
RUNNING BACK #34.

Glenn Bass on being an AFL Champion:

Craig,

It was an exciting time in my life and a Buffalo Bill. The city of Buffalo was alive with football fever.

My role as a member of the 1964-65 championship teams was unforgetable. I was glad to make a major contribution.

We remain the _only_ championship teams in Buffalo history. I have always realized that I was very fortunate.

Thanks for contacting me. May God bless you & yours-

Merry Christmas

Glenn Bass
#85

Craig,

It was an exciting time in my life and a Buffalo Bill. The city of Buffalo was alive with football fever.

My role as a member of the 1964-65 Championship teams was unforgettable. I was glad to make a major contribution.

We remain the only championship teams in Buffalo history. I have always realized that I was very fortunate.

Thanks for contacting me. May God bless you & yours.

Merry Christmas,

Glenn Bass #85

In Wilson, NC on April 12, 1939 Glenn Alden Bass was born. He attended East Carolina University in Greenville. While at ECU, Bass competed in football and baseball. He shined on the diamond where he played shortstop and was named all conference in 1961. On the gridiron Bass manned the halfback position on coach Jack Boone's Pirates squad. In 1960 he was the team captain and also had a record setting 100 yard kickoff return for a touchdown. For his exploits Glenn Bass was inducted into the East Carolina Hall Of Fame in 1974.

After Bass' Pirates career came to a close the NFL and AFL both came calling. The NFL's St. Louis Cardinals chose him in the fifth round. The San Diego Chargers of the AFL waited until round 23. He signed with the Chargers, but was traded to the Buffalo Bills before the 1961 season. Bass thrived as an offensive end under coach Lou Saban with the Bills. His rookie year he hauled in 50 passes for nearly 800 yards. During

Buffalo's first AFL Championship season in 1964, Bass had nearly 900 receiving yards and seven touchdowns. 94 of those receiving yards came on one catch accounting for the longest pass completion in the AFL that season. Glenn Bass wrapped up his professional football career with two seasons in Houston.

Red Cashion on being a Super Bowl referee:

Craig, the Super Bowl is a special game - a lot of fun -
You feel the pressure but you get ready for it
and then do your job. Hope you enjoyed watching!

Red

Craig , the Super Bowl is a special game, a lot of fun, you feel the pressure but you get ready for it then do your job. Hope you enjoyed watching!
Red

Mason L. "Red" Cashion was born in College Station, Texas in 1931. He stayed close to home and attended college at Texas A&M University. While at A&M in 1952 Cashion started officiating local high school football games. For the next two decades Red officiated college games in the Lone Star, Southland and Southwest Conferences. In 1972 Cashion became a line judge in the National Football League and was promoted to referee four seasons later. Cashion was the head referee for Super Bowls XX and XXX. During his career as a ref he became well known for his animated "First Dowwwwwwn!" calls. After he retired in 1997 Cashion served as a trainer for NFL and Big 12 Conference referees. Cashion was inducted into the Texas Sports Hall Of Fame in 1999.

Super Bowl XX featured the Chicago Bears versus the New England Patriots. Both teams were coached by Pro Football Hall Of Fame pass catchers, Chicago's Mike Ditka and New England's Raymond Berry. The 17-1 Bears and their stifling defense were favored by ten points heading into the contest. That line proved to be conservative as the Patriots lost by 36. Richard Dent was named MVP.

The Dallas Cowboys and the Pittsburgh Steelers met in Super Bowl XXX. Larry Allen intercepted two woefully errant

Neil O'Donnell passes to seal the 27-17 Dallas victory. At the time it was the most watched televised sporting event of all time.

Pat Richter on Wisconsin and the Rose Bowl:

While I was in Madison I participated in three sports - football, basketball and baseball. Although I had a chance to play professional baseball, I chose the NFL and played 8 seasons.

While at Wisconsin I received All American honors in both 1961 and 1962. I was a member of the 1962 Big Ten Championship team and we played in the 1963 Rose Bowl. That game featured #1 USC vs. #2 Wisconsin and although we were behind 42-14 early in the fourth quarter we managed to stage a rally + close the gap to 42-37 at the final gun. It was considered to be one of the most exciting sports events of all time.

Best Regards,
Pat Richter

107

While I was in Madison I participated in three sports- football, basketball and baseball. Although I had a chance to play professional baseball I chose the NFL and played 8 seasons.

Pat
RICHTER
WASH. REDSKINS • END

While at Wisconsin I received All-American honors in both 1961 and 1962. I was a member of the 1962 Big Ten Championship team and we played in the 1963 Rose Bowl. That game featured #1 USC vs. #2 Wisconsin and although we were behind 42-14 early in the fourth quarter we managed to stage a rally to close the gap to 42-37 at the final gun. It was considered to be one of the most exciting sports events of all time.

Best Regards,
Pat Richter

Pat Richter was born in Madison, WI on September 9th, 1941. He has spent a majority of his life in Madison and has accomplished much in his home town. At 6' 5" and 225 pounds Richter was the last nine time letterman in the history of the University Of Wisconsin. In the Rose Bowl he set a record with 11 catches good for 163 yards. He was chosen with the seventh pick in the first round by the Washington Redskins.

Richter was used primarily as a punter from 1963 through 1967. Richter led the league in punts and punt yardage in 1964. In 1968 he was used as a tight end and gave Hall Of Famer Sonny Jurgensen a reliable target. That season Richter had 42 receptions for 533 yards and nine touchdowns. Pat Richter retired after the 1970 season.

Richter spent the next 17 years working in the private sector before being recruited back to his alma mater. In 1989 Richter became the athletic director at the University Of Wisconsin-Madison. He inherited a program that was in two million dollars of debt, with outdated facilities and waning fan support. One of the first things he did was hire Notre Dame's defensive coordinator Barry Alvarez as the Badgers' head coach. The accomplishments of Alvarez's teams helped bring attention and financial backing to all sports in Madison. After 14 successful years, Richter stepped down as athletic director. Outside of Camp Randall Stadium, home of the Badgers, is a life sized bronze statue of Pat Richter on a large stone pedestal.

Emerson Boozer on Super Bowl III:

After Watching Three films of
The Colts, the offence felt that if
They - The Colts, played us using A 3-4 Defense
we would defeat them. The Jets defense was
NOT a part of this meeting, as the defense and
Offense meet sepuately. When the Offensive Coordinator
Turn off the Camara... There was a buzz of Chatter
in the Room from the players. COACH EUBANKS ended
The meeting by telling the offense that we were Too
cofident and would get our heads handed to us
if we continued with this attitude.
   Some times during the evening, our QB went off
Out to dinner and upon his Return, Told Reporters
That he Gurantee a Victor by the Jets on Sunday -
The Rest is history!
                                    Sincerly
                                    Emerson Boozer
                                         32

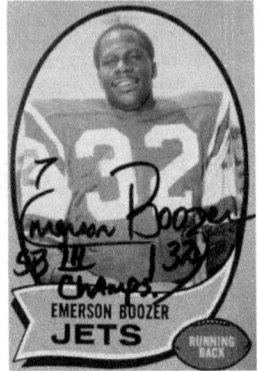

After watching three films of the Colts, the offense felt that if they- the Colts, played us using a 3-4 defense we would defeat them. The Jets defense was not part of this meeting, as the defense and offense meet separately. When the offensive coordinator turned off the camera...there was a buzz of chatter in the room from the players. Coach Ewbank ended the meeting by telling the offense that we were too confident and would get our heads handed to us if we continued with this attitude. Sometime during the evening, our QB went out to dinner and upon his return, told reporters that he guaranteed a victor by the Jets on Sunday- the rest is history!

Sincerely,

Emerson Boozer

As America celebrated its Independence Day in 1943, Emerson Boozer was born in Augusta, Georgia. While Boozer was a superb prep athlete, racial segregation in the early 1960's caused him to be lightly recruited by large conference colleges. He wound up thriving at Maryland Eastern Shore. Boozer played running back and full back for the Hawks from 1962 through 1965.

The AFL and NFL had yet to merge by the time their respective 1966 drafts rolled around. Boozer was chosen in the seventh round by the Pittsburgh Steelers in the NFL Draft and the sixth round of the AFL Draft. At that time Pro Football Hall Of Famer Weeb Ewbank was gathering talent for the Jets. He wanted hard working, enthusiastic, and talented men of any creed and color to play for the Jets. Ewbank found a man who met his requirements in Emerson Boozer.

Boozer began his professional career being compared to the great Gale Sayers. Knee injuries robbed him of his physical gifts, however Boozer adapted his game. He became a blocking back, a pass catcher and a short yardage rusher. His two Pro Bowl selections, one All Pro nod and 52 career touchdowns are a testament to his resilience over his 10 year professional career.

John Morrow on the Browns:

Dear Craig

In Cleveland we experienced great success. We had many gifted players that played well together. The world championship in 1964 was very special.

Personal Regards

John Morrow

Dear Craig,

In Cleveland we experienced great success. We had many gifted players that played well together. The World Championship in 1964 was very special.

Personal Regards,

John Morrow

Port Huron, Michigan welcomed John M. Morrow on April 27, 1933. He stayed in-state and played his college ball for College Football Hall Of Famer Bennie Oosterbaan's Michigan Wolverines. Morrow played three seasons on the varsity squad and was chosen 336th overall in the 1956 NFL Draft by the Los Angeles Rams. While he played mostly offensive tackle while he was in Ann Arbor, he was moved to center with the Rams. Morrow played 35 games over three seasons before being traded to the Cleveland Browns for Art Hunter. John Morrow had even greater success with the Browns. He played 90 consecutive games over seven seasons with the Browns. He was named to the Pro Bowl in 1961 and 1963.

The 1964 Cleveland Browns were loaded with future Pro Football Hall Of Famers. Jim Brown and Leroy Kelly manned the backfield, Gene Hickerson and Lou "The Toe" Groza anchored the offensive line and wide receiver Paul Warfield was a young deep threat. The 1964 Browns also boasted Pro Bowl quarterback Frank Ryan who led the league in touchdown passes during the regular season. The Browns needed to win the last game of the regular season to earn a berth into the NFL

Championship Game. Ryan threw five touchdown passes and ran for another one in a 52-20 rout of the New York Giants.

The 1964 NFL Championship Game pitted the 10-3-1 Browns against the 12-2 Baltimore Colts. The Browns went on to dominate the game. Frank Ryan threw three touchdown passes and Lou Groza kicked two field goals and three extra points for a 27-0 victory. The Browns also made the NFL Championship Game in 1965, but they fell to the Green Bay Packers 23-12. As of 2014 the Browns 1964 title was the last championship victory any Cleveland professional sports team has earned.

Jack "Moose" Myers on winning for Greasy Neale:

Dear Craig,

Greasy was a salty old character,
but he loved his players and
respected them.

Why wouldn't he we won him
2 world championships?

He was fun to play for as
you knew he was for you?

Good Luck
Jack "Moose" Myers

Dear Craig,
Greasy was a salty old character,
but he loved his players and respected
them. Why wouldn't he, we won him 2
World Championships! He was fun to
play for as you knew he was for you!
Good Luck
Jack "Moose" Myers

John Melvin Meyers was born on October 8th, 1924 in Saint Louis, Missouri. He went on to play college football at UCLA. Philadelphia tabbed him with the 33rd overall pick in the 1948 NFL draft. In his three seasons as a running for the Eagles, Meyers was a member of two NFL Championship teams. "Moose" finished his career as a player with the Los Angeles Rams in 1952.

Jack Meyers would follow Greasy Neale's path from the professional gridiron to the coaching ranks. In 1953 at the age of 28, Meyers became the youngest coach in Division I college football. He coached the tiny College Of Pacific, which at the time had a total enrollment of around 1,700 students. During his tenure "Moose" made sure that his teams of "Davids" took on as many "Goliaths" as possible. His very first game as coach, his Tigers played and defeated Stanford University. In 1958 his charges beat the University Of California Bears, the eventual Rose Bowl Champions. His teams also defeated Texas Tech, Brigham Young and Oregon State among others during his tenure. In 1960 the president of The College Of Pacific deemphasized the football program without discussing the matter with Meyers. Meyers left the college, ending his coaching career.

In 2007, 60 of his former players, "Moose's Men" as they call themselves gathered for Moose Meyers Weekend. One of those former players was Tom Flores. Flores was a quarterback at Pacific, played pro football and then went into coaching.

Don Dufek On The 1951 Rose Bowl:

Dear Craig

Thanks for your letter re: the '51 Rose Bowl. I'm sure you know that we won the game 14-6. and that I scored our two TD's. This was a great win for Michigan + of course we'll never forget this great Michigan Victory. As I'm sure you know — California was favored + in a sense had a home team advantage. Our victory was very satisfying and your comments are very satisfying. Best wishes + regards.

Don Dufek

Dear Craig,

Thanks for your letter re: the '51 Rose Bowl. I'm sure you know that we won the game 14-6 and that I scored our two TD's. This was a great win for Michigan and of course we'll never forget this great Michigan victory. As I'm sure you know- California was favored and in a sense had a home team advantage. Our victory was very satisfying and your comments are very satisfying.

Best wishes and regards,
Don Dufek

Don Dufek had been one of coach Bennie Oosterbaan's Wolverines since the National Championship season of 1948. When he stepped onto the field of the Rose Bowl on January 1, 1951, Dufek was the starting offensive fullback for the 1950 Big Ten Champs. The first half of the Rose Bowl, the Pacific Coast Conference Champion University Of California had dominated Michigan and led 6-0. The Bears held an advantage of 192-65 in offensive yardage and had gained 10 first downs to Michigan's two. During halftime coach Oosterbaan made adjustments to turn the tide. Michigan's defense held Cal's potent offense at bay and the teams fought to a stalemate in the third quarter. It was the fourth quarter when Dufek would run himself into the annals of Big Blue history. Dufek ran for two touchdowns and a total of 113 yards leading to a 14-6 Wolverine victory and a Rose Bowl MVP award. For his contributions during his three seasons as a letterman in football Dufek was inducted into the University Of Michigan Hall Of Honor in 2006.

Don Dufek's contributions to his alma mater did not end on New Year's Day 1951. Two of Dufek's sons, Don Jr. and Bill went on to All American careers at the University Of Michigan. A third son, Joe, played quarterback at Yale. Don Jr. played professionally for the inaugural Seattle Seahawks and Joe quarterbacked the Buffalo Bills.

Sam "Bam" Cunningham on the 1973 Rose Bowl:

Hi Craig,

The Rose Bowl was one of The Reasons I chose USC! It was Such a Great Game to watch on Jan. 1 and Seem to always have Great moments and influence on The College Football Season!

It took Three Seasons to Get There as A Player and It Lived Up to it's Reputation and more Than I had dreamed of!

We Played Ohio State in Front of 106,000 Fans. Our Team Was Very Good, They were a bit Young. Even if They Had Been Older It would not have been Too much of a Problem. That "73" Rose Bowl Team is one of The Best if not The Best Football Team I've Ever Played On!

We Finished Strong and Won The National Championship! Great memories!

Fight On!
Sam 'Bam' Cunham #39

127

Hi Craig,

The Rose Bowl was one of the reasons I chose USC! It was such a great game to watch on Jan. 1 and seemed to always have great moments and influence on the college football season.

It took three seasons to get there as a player and it lived up to its reputation and more than I had dreamed of!

SAM CUNNINGHAM   RUNNING BACK
PATRIOTS

We Played Ohio State in front of 106,000 fans. Our team was very good, they were a bit young. Even if they had been older it would not have been too much of a problem. That '73 Rose Bowl team is one of the best if not the best football team I've ever played on!

We finished strong and won the National Championship! Great Memories!

Fight on!

Sam "Bam" Cunningham

Samuel Lewis Cunningham Jr. was born in Santa Barbara, California on August 15, 1950. Cunningham became a star for the University Of Southern California in 1970. The opening game of the season pitted the USC Trojans against the Crimson Tide of the University Of Alabama. The game was played in Birmingham. Cunningham used his 6' 3" 230 lb. frame to run over, around and through the Tide's defense to the tune of 12 carries for 135 yards and two touchdowns. The Trojans crushed the perennial powerhouse Crimson Tide 42-21. More significant than a big road victory was the social ramifications that followed. Alabama's legendary head coach Paul "Bear" Bryant was one of the last coaches to recruit African-American players. It is widely believed that Cunningham's performance that day against Bryant's all white Tide was the catalyst for integration of Alabama football. Sam Cunningham was an All-American in 1972 and inducted into the College Football Hall Of Fame in 2010.

Cunningham was the 11th overall pick of the 1973 NFL Draft by the New England Patriots. During his NFL career he scored 49 total touchdowns and was named to the 1978 Pro Bowl. Sam's younger brother is former NFL star quarterback Randall Cunningham.

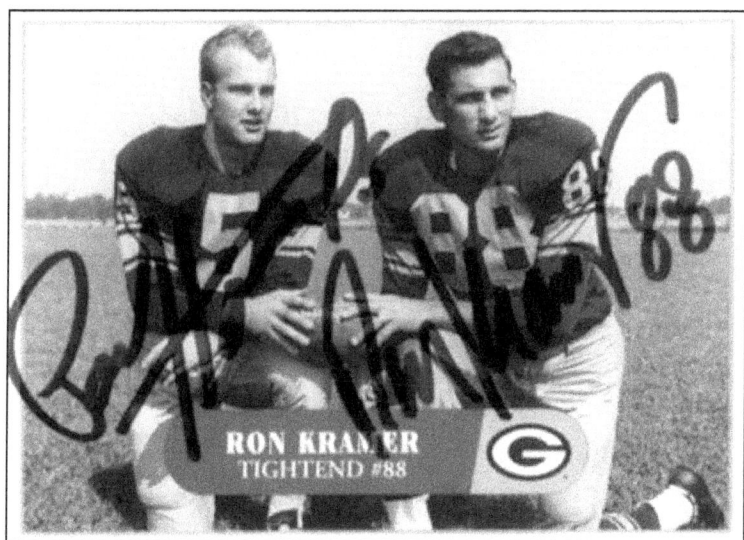

RON KRAMER
TIGHTEND #88

Mike Guman On Hall Of Famer Eric Dickerson:

Hi Craig,

Thanks for your note. Eric was not only a great football player but he was a good person as well. He in my opinion had the greatest combination of size, speed, power and aggressiveness of any back I know. I think he's in the top 5 RB's of all time.

Eric was a hard worker and great competitor & I was a pleasure blocking for him!

Sincerely

MG

Raymond Berry on Johnny Unitas:

Craig - I first met John in T'ng Camp July 1956. He had been cut By the Steelers in '55. I was returning for my 2d year with the Colts and I was to be cut after a non productive Rookie Year 1955. We hit it off immediately Because we Both loved to play footBall and were desperate to survive. We Both had strong work ethic. When practice ended we Stayed out and practiced together - I ran the route he threw the Ball - over and over and over and over. George Shaw, our starting QB, was injured early in '56 season. John came in and for the first time we were a combo. We Began to click in the games. John Began to show why he was to Become great. The man responsible for putting us on the field was Weeb Ewbank our head coach. When we were unknown nothings he saw something others didn't see and went with us.

Raymond Berry

Craig- I first met John in T'ng (training) camp July 1956. He had been cut by the Steelers in '55. I was retuning for my 2nd year with the Colts and I was to be cut after a non productive rookie year 1955. We hit it off immediately because we both loved to play football and were desperate to survive. We both had strong work ethic. When practice ended we stayed out and practiced together- I ran the route he threw the ball- over and over and over and over. George Shaw, our starting QB was injured early in '56 season. John came in and for the first time we were a combo. We began to click in the games. John began to show why he was to become great. The man responsible for putting us on the field was Weeb Ewbank, our head coach. When we were unknown nothings he saw something others didn't see and went with us.

Raymond Berry

Raymond Emmett Berry was born in Corpus Christi, TX on February 27, 1933. He was drafted out of Southern Methodist University in the 20th round of the 1954 NFL draft. 231 players were selected before the Baltimore tabbed Berry that year. Berry went on to play his entire career for the Baltimore Colts. During thirteen seasons he lost only one fumble. While participating in the "Greatest Game Ever Played", the 1958 NFL Championship,

Berry caught a record 12 passes. He was an All Pro six times and was elected to six Pro Bowls. After his playing career, Berry went on to coach in the NFL leading the New England Patriots to Super Bowl XX. For his accomplishments with the Colts Raymond Berry was enshrined in the Pro Football Hall of Fame in 1973.

Clay Matthews on Leo Nomellini:

Dear Craig—
Thanks for the note! I
enjoyed playing with Leo
for many years—
Good luck to you—
Clay Matthews
S.F. 49'ers 1950-1955

Dear Craig-

Thanks for the note! I enjoyed playing with Leo for many years. Good luck to you.

Clay Matthews S.F. 49ers 1950-1955

LEO
NOMELLINI
DEFENSIVE TACKLE · SAN FRANCISCO 49ers

William Clay Matthews was born in Charleston, South Carolina on August 1, 1928. He came from an athletic background as his father was a multiple sport coach at The Citidel. Matthews went to college at Louisiana State University where he played offensive and defensive tackle for the Tigers. He was drafted in the 25th round of the 1949 NFL Draft. Matthews went on to play for the San Francisco 49ers for four seasons. He served in the United States Army as a paratrooper in the Korean War in the middle of his playing career. After his playing career, Matthews went in to a long, successful bussiness career.

More than his playing, military and business career, Clay Matthews is famous for his offspring. Two of his children, Clay Jr. and Bruce went on to play football in college and the National Football League. Clay Jr. was a Pro Bowl linebacker and Bruce was a tackle who is a member of the Pro Football Hall Of Fame. Five of Clay Sr.'s grandsons are also fooball players. Clay III is a linebacker for Green Bay, Casey is a linebacker for Philadelphia, Kevin is a center for Tennessee, Jake is a tackle for Atlanta and

Mike plays offensive line for Texas A&M University. The Matthews brood is the largest of its kind in NFL history.

Leo Nomellini (1924-2000) had never played a down of football until he was a member of the Marines during WWII. After his discharge he was accepted an athletic scholarship at the University Of Minnesota where he was named consensus All-America for the 1948 and 1949 seasons . Nomellini was the first ever draft pick of the San Francisco 49ers. He played every game at offensive and defensive lineman for 14 seasons for the Niners. During his career he was named All-Pro nine times and was picked to ten Pro Bowls. Nomellini was inducted into the Pro Football Hall Of Fame in 1969 and the College Football Hall Of Fame in 1977.

Marv Montgomery on Floyd Little:

I enjoyed blocking for Floyd. He was one of the quickest backs in the league. It was also my job to get downfield on the off side because you knew that once Floyd got in the secondary that he was probably coming your way dodging tackles. I was happy that he was inducted into the Hall of fame He deserved it

Best Wishes
Marv Montgomery

Craig Sievers

I enjoyed blocking for Floyd. He was one of the quickest backs in the league. It was also my job to get down field on the off side because you knew that once Floyd got in the secondary that he was probably coming your way dodging tackles. I was happy that he was inducted into the Hall Of Fame. He deserved it.

Best Wishes, Marv Montgomery

FLOYD LITTLE • RB

MARV MONTGOMERY | TACKLE
BRONCOS

Marvin Montgomery was born in Torrance, CA on February 8, 1948. After two years at Los Angeles City College Montgomery moved on the University Of Southern California. While playing tackle for the Trojans, he helped open running lanes for Clarence Davis to rush for over 2,300 yards over two seasons. The Trojans won the 56th Anniversary Rose Bowl in 1970 by defeating the Michigan Wolverines by a touchdown. The Denver Broncos made Montgomery the 12th overall pick of the 1971 National Football League Draft. He played five seasons at left tackle for the Broncos. Montgomery started 32 of the 57 games he played for Denver. He played two seasons with the New Orleans Saints and one with the Atlanta Falcons before retiring from the NFL. He returned to the Denver area after his playing days and embarked on a successful career in business.

Floyd Little (1942-) played his college ball at Syracuse University. Like Jim Brown and Ernie Davis before him, Little wore the famous #44 jersey for the Orangemen. He was three times named All-America. 1967 marked the first AFL-NFL common draft. Prior to that time, the two leagues had separate drafts and fought to sign players drafted by both. The Broncos selected Little with the 6th overall pick. In Denver he not only continued to wear the number 44, he also continued his success carrying the football. Over his nine seasons Little rushed for 6,323 yards which at the time of his retirement ranked sixth all time in NFL history. Floyd Little was inducted into the College Football Hall Of Fame in 1983, the Denver Broncos Ring Of Fame in 1984 and the Pro Football Hall Of Fame in 2010.

Don McIlhenny on Paul Hornung and Jim Taylor:

Paul & Jimmy were great players —
both in NFL Hall of fame — great teammates and life long friends

Don McIlhenny

Paul and Jimmy were great players-both in the NFL Hall Of Fame- great teammates and lifelong friends.

Don McIlhenny

Donald Brookes McIlhenny was born on November 22, 1934 in Cleveland, OH. He played his college ball at Southern Methodist University where he was a three time letterman at halfback. Detroit drafted McIlhenny three picks ahead of Hall Of Famer Sam Huff in the third round of the 1956 NFL Draft. During his one season in the Motor City, McIlhenny shared the backfield with former Heisman Trophy winners Leon Hart and Howard Cassidy. McIlhenny went to Green Bay in 1957 and traded Heisman winners for Hall Of Famers. He spent three seasons with the Packers accounting for over 1,300 yards of total offense and seven touchdowns. The newly formed Dallas Cowboys chose McIlhenny in the 1960 NFL Expansion Draft. He lined up behind Eddie LeBaron on September, 24th 1960 as the first running back in Dallas Cowboys history. He spent a season and a half with Dallas and finished his career with five games with the 49ers.

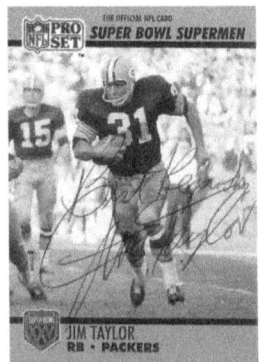

Paul Hornung (1935-) spent his entire nine season NFL career with the Green Bay Packers. After winning the Heisman Trophy in 1956, the "Golden Boy" was the first overall pick in the 1957 NFL draft. The Packers won three NFL Championships and one Super Bowl during Hornung's tenure with the team. Hornung, along with Detroit's star defensive lineman Alex Karras, was suspended for the 1963 season for gambling on NFL games. After promising to stay out of Las Vegas, commissioner Pete Rozelle reinstated both stars for the 1964 season. Hornung was inducted into the Pro Football Hall Of Fame in 1986.

Jim Taylor (1935-) was born and raised in Baton Rouge, LA and played his college ball at Louisiana State University. He was an All American with the Bayou Bengals and was drafted in the second round of the 1958 NFL Draft. He was a five time Pro Bowler and four time champion with the Packers. He was elected to the Pro Football Hall Of Fame in 1976.

John Vella on his Raiders teammates:

CRAIG,

To be a Raider in the 70's was the best. Great players great personalities. My rookie year we had offensive line vets that were willing to help rookies like myself & #50 Dave Dalby. Vets like Upshaw, Shell, Bob Brown, Ron Mix, Jim Otto, George Buehler. All great players all willing to help rookies. The experience of playing w/ the Raiders was one that we felt we could win every time we went on the field. Beating Steelers in AFC Championship and Vikings in S.Bowl XI definite high points in my career.

My best,

John Vella

Craig,

To be a Raider in the 70's was the best. Great players, great personalities. My rookie year we had offensive line vets that were willing to help rookies like myself & #50 Dave Dalby. Vets like Upshaw, Shell, Bob Brown, Ron Mix, Jim Otto, George Buehler. All great players willing to help rookies. The experience of playing with the Raiders was one that we felt we could win every time we went on the field. Beating the Steelers in the AFC Championship and the Vikings in Super Bowl XI, definite high points in my career.

My Best,
John Vella

John Vella was born in Cleveland, OH on April 21, 1950. He attended Notre Dame High School in Sherman Oaks, CA. He stayed in-state for his collegiate career and attended the University Of Southern California. While at USC Vella played offensive tackle and was named All-America in 1971. He stayed in California once again when Oakland chose him in the second round of the NFL Draft. Vella became part of the golden age of Oakland Raider football.

The 1976 Oakland Raiders offensive line is regarded as one of the greatest in the history of professional football. The Raiders finished the regular season with a record of 13-1 with their only loss coming in a week four drubbing at the hands of the Patriots in New England. The Raiders had home field advantage for the playoffs and in the first round got revenge beating the Patriots. It got no easier in the AFC Championship Game as the Pittsburgh Steelers and their vaunted "Steel Curtain" defense visited the Oakland Coliseum. Vella and his line mates held the Steelers to two quarterback sacks allowing Ken Stabler to throw two touchdowns en route to victory. There was no rest for the Raiders' linemen as they met the NFC Champion Minnesota Vikings in Super Bowl XI. The Vikings defensive line was known as "The Purple People Eaters" and boasted two future Hall Of Famers in Carl Eller and Alan Page. Once again Stabler was only sacked twice and Raider runners combined for 266 yards and two touchdowns. Oakland won the Super Bowl 32-14. Vella played for the Raiders through the 1979 season.

After retiring from the NFL he owned and operated "John Vella's Raider Locker Room". His store sold only Raider memorabilia and was open from 1987 through 2003.

Gary Fencik on practicing against Walter Payton:

Walter was great to practice against because few backs had his moves which made playing in a game easier than practicing

Gary Fencik
45

Walter was great to practice against because few backs had his moves which made playing in a game easier than practicing.

Gary Fencik 45

John Gary Fencik was born June 11, 1954 in Chicago, Illinois. He went to college at Yale University and played wide receiver on the football squad. In 1976 the Miami Dolphins chose Fencik with the 281st pick in the NFL Draft and switched him to defensive back. Fencik ruptured his lung while securing a tackle during a scrimmage against the Saints before the season. By the time he was ready to return to the field there was no room on Miami's roster. Chicago picked Fencik up after the first week of the regular season and he went on to play 164

games over twelve seasons. Over his career he was named All-Pro and Pro Bowler twice each. He was a key member of Buddy Ryan's "46 Defense". When Fencik retired after the 1987 season he was the Bears all-time leader in interceptions with 38.

Walter Payton (1954-1999) was born in Columbia, Mississippi. He was an excellent athlete and student at Jefferson High School. Although racial tensions by the early 1970's had lessened opportunities for black student athletes in the south were still limited. Payton was one of the best half backs in the Mississippi he did not receive a single scholarship offer from a

Southeastern Conference school. Walter Payton joined his brother Eddie and went to college at Jackson State University . During his four years as a Tiger, Payton rushed 598 times for 3,563 yards scoring 63 touchdowns. He also handled the place kicking duties.

Payton was chosen with the fourth pick in the 1975 NFL Draft. He led the League in carries four out of his first five pro seasons and led in rushing yards with 1,852 in 1977. Payton was named to nine Pro Bowls and was named All-Pro nine times. He was the NFL Most Valuable Player in 1976, 1977 and 1985. Payton set the career rushing record with 16,726 yards and the rushing touchdown record with 110. He could have accumulated significantly more yards and TDs had there not been two strike shortened seasons during his career. Payton was inducted into the College Football Hall Of Fame and the Pro Football Hall Of Fame.

Dave Herman on Joe Namath:

To Craig -

Joe was just saying what the entire team felt -
We could and would win!!!

It was Joe's quote of our thoughts

there is only one quarterback ---.!
for gosh

Dave Herman

N Y Jets (1964 - 1973)
#67

To Craig,

Joe was just saying what the entire team felt- we could and would win!!!

It was Joe's quote of our thoughts. There is only on quarterback for quotes!

Dave Herman NY Jets 1964-1973 #67

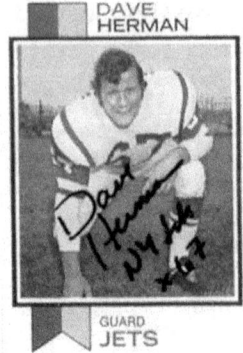

David Jon Herman was born in Bryan, Ohio on September 3, 1941. He chose to leave the great state of Ohio and play his college ball at Michigan State University. After Herman's college career he was chosen 211th overall in the 1963 AFL draft by the New York Jets. Players drafted that late were usually long shots to make a team's active roster. Herman made the team and appeared in five contests as a rookie. By his second season he was the starting right offensive guard. He played nine professional seasons all with the Jets and was named an AFL All-Star twice.

While it was Joe Namath who got most of the attention before the Super Bowl and the MVP award after it, Herman may have had the biggest hand in the victory. In 1969, after five seasons of starting Herman at guard, coach Weeb Ewbank moved him to tackle. Sam Walton was a rookie and had been starting at right tackle since the first game of the regular season. However toward the end of the season Walton began to falter. The Jets were set to face the Oakland Raiders in the AFL Championship Game. During the regular season Oakland's Ike Lassiter had dominated Walton contributing to a Jets defeat. With Herman in Walton's position the Jets were able to neutralize the Raider pass rush and win 17-7.

Before Super Bowl III Ewbank decided to go with Herman at tackle again. The Baltimore Colts had one of the most feared pass rushers in all of professional football, Bubba Smith. Smith had been the number one overall draft pick in the 1967. While Smith had six inches and 30 pounds on him, Herman was able to stifle the big defensive end. His performance helped give Namath the time and Matt Snell the running lanes to defeat the heavily favored Colts 16-7.

Paul Wiggin on Jim Brown:

Both Paul Brown and Blanton Collier were believers in protecting their skill players so — I have never tackled Jim. Every other part of our practice tempo was "full go". Modernly that practice tempo is called "thud". During my 11 years with the Browns, the first 9 were with Jim and his role was the belief factor that we all felt just having him as a teammate which was always reinforced by his play on Sunday. We never had a losing season in my 11 seasons (Leroy Kelly was "the man" my last two years)

Paul W.

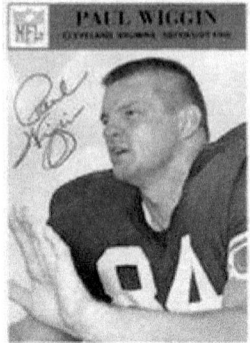

Both Paul Brown and Blanton Collier were believers in protecting their skill players so I have never tackled Jim. Every other part of our practice tempo was "full go". Modernly that practice tempo is called "thud". During my 11 years with the Browns, the first 9 were with Jim and his role was the belief factor that we all felt just having him as a teammate which was always reinforced by his play on Sunday. We never had a losing season in my 11 seasons. (Leroy Kelly was "The Man" my last two years)

Paul Wiggin

Paul David Wiggin was born on November 18, 1934 in Modesto, CA. He was a standout defensive tackle at Stanford University where he was twice named first team All American. Wiggin was inducted into the College Football Hall Of Fame in 2005.

Wiggin was drafted in the 6th round of the 1956 NFL draft by the Cleveland Browns. Wiggin spent his entire eleven year career with Cleveland. He never missed a regular season contest as a Brown, participating in all of 146 possible games. In 1964, Wiggin was a key member of one of the stingiest defenses in the National Football League. The Browns won ten games during the regular season and earned the right to face the Baltimore Colts in the NFL Championship Game on December 27, 1964. Don Shula's Colts led the NFL in scoring offense in 1964. Baltimore boasted Hall Of Famers Johnny Unitas, John Mackey, Lenny Moore, Jim Parker and Raymond Berry. Wiggin and his mates on defense held the high flying Colts scoreless and won the NFL Championship 27-0. Wiggin was named to two Pro Bowl squads during his tenure.

Paul Wiggin went into coaching immediately following his playing career. He spent over two decades on NFL and college sidelines as a coach. Wiggin was the coach of his alma mater from 1980 through 1983. His quarterback during that time was future Hall Of Famer John Elway.

Bill Bain on hitting and Eric Dickerson:

DEAR MR. SEVERS, it was a time that you left in the MORNING + AFTERNOON practice during camp EVERYDAY for 6 weeks ADD THAT up for 12 yrs ALOT of HITS, THEN GAMES + practice AT LEAST 2 MORE HITTING days A WEEK ADD THAT up. AND if you got HURT NO SALARY cap they just went out + got someone else off the street. The good that comes from Hitting is that 20-30 yrs from when you played you run into someone you played with and a INSTANT Bond comes back to Life, that's A NICE FEELING I get + HURT NOW w/ ERIC DICKERSON once a year after HIS Rookie [1808] record 1983 + NFL Rushing Record 1984 2105 are Secure for both Years, he writes me + THANK me. Ø THANK Him FOR EVEN THINKING I am PART of (HIS) record. A Very Humble + NICE MAN ERIC IS!

                                        BILL
                                        BAIN

165

Dear Mr. Sievers, it was a time that you hit in the morning & afternoon practice during camp everyday for 6 months. Add that up for 12 years a lot of hits. Then games & practice. At least 2 more hitting days a week. Add that up and you got hurt.

No salary cap they just went out & got someone else off the street. The good that came from hitting is that 20-30 years from when you played you run into someone you played with and an instant bond comes back to life, that's a nice feeling.

I get that now w/ Eric Dickerson once a year after his rookie 1808 (yds) record 1983 & NFL Rushing Record 1984 2105 (yds) are secure for another year, he writes me & thanks me. I thank him for even thinking I am part of HIS record. A very humble & nice man Eric is!

Bill Bain

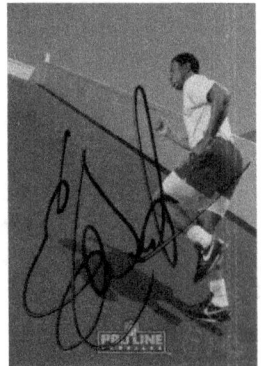

William Ernest Bain Was born in Los Angeles, CA on August 9, 1952. Bill played his college ball at the University Of Southern California and was an All American in 1974. Bain was a member of two USC National Championship teams in 1972 and 1974. In the 1975 NFL Draft the Green Bay Packers selected Bain in the second round. He would play eleven seasons in the League with five different teams: The Packers, Broncos, Rams,

Patriots and Jets. Bain had his most success as a member of the Los Angeles Rams. He played 96 games for Los Angeles starting 41.

Eric Dickerson (1960-) was a star at Southern Methodist University during the Mustangs' very turbulent era of the early 1980's. In what would go down as the greatest quarterback draft in NFL history, the running back was the second overall pick in the 1983. Dickerson was an immediate sensation as a rookie runner for the Los Angeles Rams. As of the beginning of the 2014 season his rookie rushing record still stands. His second season was even more incredible setting the single season rushing record that also remains. The Rams traded Dickerson to the Indianapolis Colts three games into the 1987 season. The trade would go down as one of the largest in terms of players and draft choices involved. During eleven NFL seasons he amassed over thirteen thousand rushing yards. Dickerson was elected to the Pro Football Hall Of Fame in 1999.

Jamie Williams on Warren Moon:

Warren was a catalyst in breaking the "myth" that a QB of color could not be successful and lead an NFL team. He was a guy of integrity, but dealt with tremendous internal and external pressure. Nevertheless, he was a superb teammate, who made himself into a Hall of Fame NFL QB. Off the field, we "broke bread" together often. Warren Moon is one of the great ones. I was honored to catch a lot of his passes!

Dr. Williams

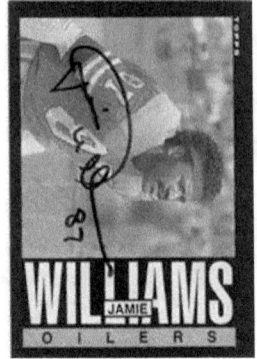

Warren was a catalyst in breaking the "myth" that a QB of color could <u>not</u> be successful and lead an NFL team. He was a guy of integrity, but dealt with tremendous internal and external pressure. Nevertheless, he was a superb teammate, who made himself into a Hall Of Fame NFL QB. Off the field we "broke bread" together often, Warren Moon is one of the great ones. I was honored to catch a lot of his passes.

Dr. Williams

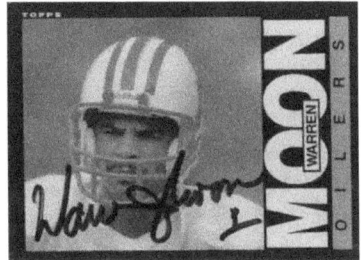

Jamie Earl Williams was born in Vero Beach, FL on February 25, 1960. Williams played his college ball for the legendary coach Tom Osborne at the University Of Nebraska. During his time in Lincoln he was a four year letter winner, named to two All Big Eight teams and was a member of two Big Eight Champion Cornhusker squads. He was inducted into the Nebraska Football Hall Of Fame in 1993. Williams was drafted by the New York Giants in the third round of the 1983 NFL Draft. He accumulated 1980 yards on 181 receptions including 11 touchdowns for his career. Williams earned a Super Bowl ring with the San Francisco 49ers. After his playing days, Williams was the athletic director of the Academy Of Art University in San Francisco. During his six years there he helped create the athletic department for the Urban Warriors as there had not been sports program at the school. Williams has since returned to Lincoln and is now a member of the Cornhuskers' athletic department as the Associate Athletic Director of Diversity and Leadership.

Warren Moon (1956-) attended the University Of Washington and played quarterback for the Huskies. He was the MVP of the 1978 Rose Bowl where he accounted for three touchdowns in a victory over Michigan. Moon went undrafted in the 1978 NFL draft so he signed with the Edmonton Eskimos of the Canadian Football League. He led the Eskimos to an unprecedented five consecutive Grey Cup Championships from 1978 through 1982. The Houston Oilers won the sweepstakes for Moon's services after his time in Canada. With the Oilers' "run and shoot" offense, Moon put up nearly 34,000 passing yards in ten seasons. In total, Moon played 17 NFL seasons. He was named to the Pro Bowl nine times and inducted into the Hall Of Fame in 2006.

Ron East on Deacon Jones and Bob Lilly:

Hi Craig - When I First saw Deacon we were Scrimmaging The Rams AT Fullerton California His reputation preceeded Him - Very quick off The Ball and He has such long legs He Shuffled Them and could cover ground very Fast in Fact I saw him Run down The QB's on The Right Side of The Field After Flushing Them out of The pocket. He didn't have much Discipline But his instinct s&Natural ability were Pretty Amazing. He Told me he never planned Any Thing Before The Ball Snap. He was Another of my mentors - 1st was Bob Lilly, I was with The Cowboys First Then The Chargers where I played with Deacon. I was Fortunate To play beside Both!

my Best Ron East

Hi Craig, When I first saw Deacon we were scrimmaging the Rams at Fullerton California. His reputation preceded him- very quick off the ball and he has such long legs he shuffled them and could cover ground very fast. In fact I saw him run down the QB's on the right side of the field after flushing them out of the pocket. He didn't have much discipline but his instincts and natural ability were pretty amazing. He told me he never planned anything before the ball snap. He was another of my mentors, 1st was Bob Lilly, I was with the Cowboys first then the Chargers where I played with Deacon. I was fortunate to play beside both!

My Best, Ron East

RON EAST | DEFENSIVE TACKLE
CHARGERS

Deacon Jones *Los Angeles Rams*

Ronald Allan East was born on August 26, 1943 in Portland Oregon. He played college football for the Bobcats of Montana State. Despite being an All-Big Sky Conference defensive lineman, East went undrafted in 1967. He caught on with the Dallas Cowboys and by the time the 1967 NFL season began he was in the defensive tackle rotation with Jethro Pugh and Bob Lilly. For four seasons East was a valuable backup for

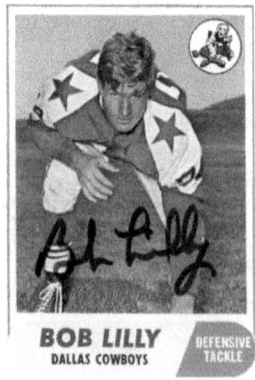

BOB LILLY | DEFENSIVE TACKLE
DALLAS COWBOYS

Tom Landry's defensive front. When the 1970 season came to a close East requested he be traded to a team where he could fight for a starting job. He was packaged in a trade that sent him to San Diego in exchange for Hall Of Famer Lance Alworth. East started 36 of the 39 games in which he participated in his three seasons in San Diego. After his playing career, Ron East returned to the pacific northwest where he has been a successful real estate developer.

David Jones (1938-2013) gave himself the nickname "Deacon" to set himself apart from all the other David Joneses in the world. As it turns out his play set him apart from everyone no matter the name. Jones went to Mississippi Valley State University and was drafted in the 14th round of the 1961 NFL Draft. Jones went on to terrify opposing quarterbacks for fourteen seasons. Jones coined the term "sack", which has since 1982 been an official stat in the NFL.

Texas Christian University's Bob Lilly (1939-) was the first ever Dallas Cowboys draft pick. He went on to be the cornerstone of Tom Landry's "Doomsday Defense". He played his entire fourteen year career with Dallas earning him the nickname "Mr. Cowboy".

Jim Cadile on Gale Sayers and Brian Piccolo:

Craig,

I was a wide rec & defensive end at San Jose State. I was drafted in the 4th round. My hopes were to play def. end or wide receiver but George Halas, on the first day of practice Halas called me over and said, Cadile, jump in there at right guard. And that was that. I had 11 years. In my early years I was 6.3 1/4" and 238 lbs. I built my weight up to two hundred & fifty.

Gale Sayers would always say nice block Jimmy on the way back to the huddle.

I was very sad when we lost Brian Piccolo. I would always be close to him. Brian & I were both Italian and we would cook together. It broke my heart when Gale was busted up. It's a rough game. George Halas was a very tough man. When he gave and order, it would be done quickly.

Best wishes Jim Cadile #72

Craig,

I was a wide rec. & defensive end at San Jose State. I was drafted in the 4th round. My hopes were to play def. end or wide receiver but George Halas, on the first day of practice called me over and said, Cadile jump in there at right guard and that was that. I had 11 years. In my early years I was 6' 3" $^{1/4}$ ft. and 238 lbs. I built my weight up to two hundred & fifty. Gale Sayers would always say nice block Jimmy on the way back to the huddle.

I was very sad when we lost Brian Piccolo. I would always be close to him. Brian & I were both Italian and we would cook together. It broke my heart when Gale was busted up. It's a rough game.

George Halas was a very tough man. When he gave an order, it would be done quickly.

Best wishes,

Jim Cadile #72

James Cadile was born in San Jose California in 1940. He was drafted by the Chicago Bears in the 4th round of the 1962 draft, 49th overall. Cadile was a guard on the 1963 NFL Championship winning Bears squad. He participated in 128 games over ten NFL seasons, all with Chicago.

Two time college All-American Gale Sayers was known as the "Kansas Comet". He was the fourth overall pick in the 1965 NFL Draft out of the University Of Kansas. The Bears were rewarded immediately for using their first draft selection on

Sayers. During his rookie campaign he accounted for 1374 yards from scrimmage and an NFL rookie record 22 total touchdowns. A brutal knee injury cut Sayers professional career short. During just seven NFL seasons, Sayers accomplished enough to be inducted into the Pro Football Hall Of Fame in 1977 on the first ballot.

Brian Piccolo was an undrafted free agent out of Wake Forrest University. He made the Bears as a special teams performer and eventually earned a role as Sayers' back up at running back. Piccolo died for embryonal cell carcinoma in 1970 at the age of 26. His friendship with Gale Sayers was the inspiration for the TV movie "Brian's Song".

COACHES

HANK STRAM
CBS

PRO SET · NFL COLLECTIBLE

Smokey Stover on Hank Stram:

Dear Craig,   Feb.6,2014

Sorry being so slow in my response.

This is how I viewed Coach Stram. I played 7yrs. for Hank. From the conception of the
AFL(1960) through the 1st Super Bowl.(1967). There is not enough adjectives to described
this man. He was not only a great coach, but a very moral, respective and upright Christian.

He had a tremendous football mind. We as a team were way ahead of the period of 3 yards
and a cloud of dust. He was an innovator of not only offensive, but defensive also.
Offensively we were running spreads and all kinds of different sets. Defensively we ran
basely the 4-3 defense, with variations. I believe we were the 1st team to have linebackers
covering the tight ends. Stram also came up with what we called the 4-4 stack. This was a
defensive that no one had seen before.

I really respected Hank, one thing that I learned from him and still carry with me through life
and business is how he handled people (players). He never ever <u>belittled</u> or <u>criticized</u> you in
front of the team. He would chew the team out not calling any names but you knew who he
was talking about. He would call you to his office one on one and buddy did he let you have
it. I have been there and done that. Upon leaving his office he would put his arm around
your shoulders and start talking to you about the next game how we were going do some
different things. Always asked about your family and kids. He would pick you right up off the
ground.

Your truly,

Smokey Stover L.B.

#35
Dallas Texans. 1960-1962
Kansas City Chiefs, 1963-1966
  AFL Champs 1962 & 1966
  1st Super Bowl 1967

CFL #25
Hamilton Tigercats 1967
Grey Cup Champs 1967

Chris Hanburger on George Allen:

THE BEST HEAD
COACH THAT I PLAYED FOR.
HIGHLY ORGANIZED. A GREAT
DEFENSIVE SYSTEM THAT WE
CONTROLED ON THE FIELD.
NO SIGNALS FROM THE
SIDLINE. WE COULD USE
ANY DEFENSE IN OUR SYSTEM
AND AUDIBLIZE AT ANY
TIME

#55

HOF 2011

The best head coach that I played for. Highly organized. A great defensive system that we controlled on the field. No signals from the sideline. We could use any defense in our system and audiblize at any time.
Chris Hanburger #55
HOF 2011

Christian G. Hanburger Jr. was born in Fort Bragg, NC on August 14th, 1941. He went on to play his college ball at the University of North Carolina. During the 1965 NFL draft 244 picks passed before the Washington Redskins tabbed Hanburger with the seventh pick of the 18th round. Despite his late draft position he started immediately at outside linebacker for the Redskins defense. He manned that position for 14 seasons. "The Hangman" was chosen to nine Pro Bowls and was named All Pro four times. In 2011 he was inducted into the Pro Football Hall of Fame after being nominated by the veterans committee.

George Allen (1918-1990) was a football coach for 42 of the 72 years of his life. Allen began his coaching career in 1948 with the Morningside College Chiefs and finished in 1990 with the Long Beach State 49ers. In between Allen earned a reputation as an extremely hard worker and stickler for detail. During his

twelve years as a head coach in the National Football League Allen coached the Los Angeles Rams and the Washington Redskins. Both teams had been perennial sub-.500 teams prior to Allen's arrival. In his five seasons with the Los Angeles the Rams posted a .742 winning percentage. In seven seasons in D.C. the Redskins had 67 wins against 30 losses and a victory in the 1972 NFC Championship. Though they were one point favorites in Super Bowl VII Allen, Hanburger and the rest of the Redskins fell to the Miami Dolphins by a touchdown. In 1992 Deacon Jones presented Coach Allen to the Pro Football Hall Of Fame.

Bill Mackrides on Greasy Neale:

I enjoyed playing for Coach Neal because he was a good coach. He knew football and was a strong instructor. We had good equipment at that time, not always brand new, replaced when needed.

We beat the Chicago Bears for the first time while I was in at quarterback and I frequently called my own plays.

Thank you for your interest!

Bill Mackrides

(dictated by Bill Mackrides
and written by his daughter-in-law)
signed by Bill Mackrides

I enjoyed playing for coach Neal(e) because he was a good coach. He knew football and was a strong instructor. We had good equipment at that time, not always brand new, replaced when needed.

We beat the Chicago Bears for the first time while I was in at quarterback and I frequently called my own plays.

Thank you for your interest!

Bill Mackrides

(dictated by Bill Mackrides and written by his daughter in law)

signed by Bill Mackrides

William Mackrides was born in Philadelphia in 1925. He attended the University of Nevada-Reno and was selected in the 3rd round of the 1947 draft by his hometown Eagles. Playing quarterback and wearing #39, Mackrides was a member of two NFL Championship squads while with Philadelphia. He split his final season between the Pittsburgh Steelers and New York Giants.

Alfred "Greasy" Neale (1891-1973) played professional football for three seasons. He spent the 1917 season playing on the Canton Bulldogs with Jim Thorpe. Neale played eight seasons in the Major Leagues roaming the outfield mostly with the Cincinnati Reds. Batting .357 for the series, he was a

member of the winning side of the 1919 World Series topping the Chicago "Black Sox". During and following his playing career Neale coached football at the college and pro level for 35 seasons. As a head coach he led Washington & Jefferson College to the 1922 Rose Bowl. Neale was the third ever coach of the Philadelphia Eagles and led them to back to back NFL Championships in 1948 and 1949. For his exploits as a coach he was inducted into the College Football Hall of Fame in 1967 and the Pro Football Hall of Fame in 1969.

Michael Downs On Tom Landry:

Craig,

Playing for Coach Landry was one of the best experiences of my life. Landry was the most consistant individuals I've known. He had no good or bad days. Each day was the same. His players responded to his demeanor. We knew what he expected and we tried to give Coach what he expected from each of us.

By the time I arrived, Coach Landry already was a legend. He created the "Flex defense". The defense's foundation was all about recognition; reading, then adjusting to the offense. If a player couldn't "read and adjust," that player didn't play.

Offensively, he had the 'quarterback shot gun' before it was fashionable. Draws and screen plays were some of his specialty.

History will show that he was before his time.

Michael Downs

Craig Sievers

Craig,

Playing for Coach Landry was one of the best experiences of my life. Landry was the most consistent individual I've known. He had no good or bad days. Each day was the same. His players responded to his demeanor. We knew what he expected and we tried to give Coach what he expected each of us. By the time I arrived, Coach Landry already was a legend. He created the "Flex Defense". The defense's foundation was all about recognition; reading, then adjusting to the offense. If a player couldn't "read and adjust," that player didn't play. Offensively, he had the "quarterback shot gun" before it was fashionable. Draws and screen plays were some of his specialty.

MICHAEL DOWNS

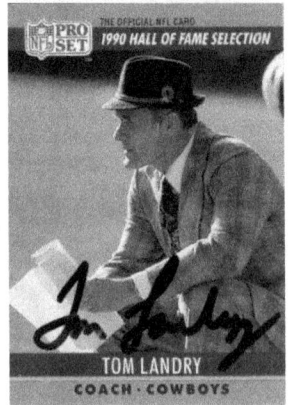

TOM LANDRY
COACH·COWBOYS

History will show that he was before his time.
Michael Downs

On June 9, 1959 Michael Lynn Downs was born in Dallas, TX. After graduating from South Oak Cliff High in Dallas Downs left Dallas for Houston and attended Rice University. He graduated with a BA in Business Management, Political Science and Physical Education. Despite being team captain, All Southwestern Conference and All-America honorable mention

Downs was not chosen in the 1981 NFL Draft. He signed with the Dallas Cowboys as a free agent and immediately started as a rookie. Michael Downs started at free safety for eight seasons and had 35 career interceptions to go along with 14 fumble recoveries. He was a team captain for the Cowboys for two seasons.

Tom Landry (1924-2000) was an All Pro player before he was an iconic coach. A University Of Texas product, Landry was drafted in the 20th round of the 1947 NFL draft by the New York Giants. He played defensive back for seven seasons and in 1954 was named to the Pro Bowl. The final two years Landry spent with the Giants he was a player/assistant coach. It was during this time that he invented the 4-3 defense that is common today. In 1960 Landry was hired as the first head coach of the expansion Dallas Cowboys. He coached the Cowboys for 29 seasons including Super Bowl winning squads in 1971 and 1977. Landry was inducted into the Pro Football Hall Of Fame in 1990.

Ed Sharkey on Ray Flaherty:

He was a very fair man and an exilent Coach

Ed. Sharkey

Craig Sievers

He was a very fair man and an excellent coach.

Ed Sharkey

Edward Joseph Sharkey was born in Brooklyn, NY on July 6, 1927. He played his college ball for Duke University and the University Of Nevada-Reno. In 1947 Sharkey joined Ray Flaherty with the New York Yankees of the All American Football Conference. When that league folded he played for five different NFL clubs including the inaugural Baltimore Colts club in 1953. Sharkey played in a third professional football league joining the British Columbia Lions of the Canadian Football League to finish his career in 1957.

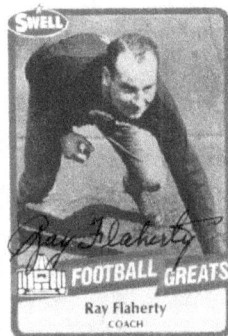

Ray Flaherty (1903-1994) joined professional football in its infancy. He played defensive and offensive end beginning in 1926 with the Los Angeles Wildcats of the short lived, first incarnation of the American Football League. From there Flaherty joined the fledgling National Football League playing two seasons with the New York Yankees and six seasons with the New York Giants. He was a member of the 1934 NFL Champion Giants and was named All-Pro three times during his playing career.

Flaherty made a seamless transition from the field to the sideline as he took over as head coach of the Boston Redskins in 1936. Under his guidance the 'Skins won two NFL

Championships. Flaherty served honorably in World War II and coached four seasons with the AAFC before retiring. He is credited with inventing the screen pass and specialized substitutions. For his accomplishments and innovations as a coach Ray Flaherty was inducted into the Pro Football Hall Of Fame in 1976.

Tommy Brooker on Bear Bryant:

I came when he came to the U of A in '58
my group came in the summer & he had his first spring prior
to our arrival. As a freshman group we could not play back
then, so we went against the varsity team every day. Prior to LSU
game on a wet, soggy Saturday we beat the varsity in a muddy
& sloppy field (Carnie Radle) was the coach in charge. Coach Bryant
came back from a scouting trip found out we beat the varsity &
he almost came unglued, could not believe we even practiced.
They almost beat LSU till the stands fell in at field in Mobile
Al! LSU goes on that year to win the National Championship!

Coach Bryant was well organized and detailed, asking us
to perform each & every day to our maximum, and if not
come back the next day & put out 110% making up for the day before,
demanding the best, writing your mama's and daddys, holding
your head high, run on & off the field, plenty of time after a
game to hug your sweetie & folks.

He traveled in class, jackets & slacks, looking great
& neat and on a team, we showed our class everywhere
we went. We worked hard and did those little things coach
told us to do our very first meeting as freshmen and
sure enough our 4th year we became the National Champion!

I played both ways, right offensive end and left defensive
end and handled the kicking duties. Kicking field goals
against Auburn in 1959 & 60 for victories (no pats in 60)
Brooker Boots Bama to Blue Bonnett Bowl was the headline
in the B'ham paper. Winning the national championship
makes you realize that you have accomplished something
that most that play the game will never accomplish that,
and it is something no one can take away from you,
ever!! I quote coach Bryant almost everyday even after
55 years later, after meeting coach Bryant. He was a
strong influence on many lives and we have another
Bryant in Nick Saban thank goodness. Roll Tide Brooker

I came when he came to the U of A in '58. My group came in the summer and he had his first spring prior to our arrival. As a freshman group we could not play back then, so we went against the varsity team every day. Prior to LSU game on a wet, soggy Saturday we beat the varsity in a muddy sloppy field (Carnie Leslie) was the coach in charge. Coach Bryant came back from a scouting trip found out we beat the varsity and he almost came unglued, could not believe we even practiced.

TOMMY BROOKER end

They almost beat LSU till the stands fell in at the field in Mobile AL! LSU goes on that year to win the National Championship!

Coach Bryant was well organized and detailed, asking us to perform each & every day to our maximum and if not come back the next day & put out 110% making up for the day before, demanding the best, writing your mammas and daddys, holding your head high on and off the field, plenty of time after a game to hug your sweetie and folks.

We travelled in class, jackets & slacks, looking great & neat and as a team we showed our class everywhere we went. We worked hard and did those little things Coach told us to do our very first meeting as freshmen and sure enough our 4th year we became the National Champions!

I played both ways, right offensive end and left defensive end and handled the kicking duties. Kicking field goals against Auburn in 1959 & '60 for victories (no pads in '60) Brooker Boots Bama to Blue Bonnet Bowl was the headline in the paper.

Winning the National Championship makes you realize that you have accomplished something that most that play the game will never accomplish that, and it is something no one can take away from you, ever!!

I quote Coach Bryant almost every day even after 55 years later, after meeting Coach Bryant. He was a strong influence on many lives and we have another Bryant in Nick Saban thank goodness.

Roll Tide,
Tommy Brooker

Ed Henke on Jimmy Phelan:

CRAIG →

1949 WAS A LONG TIME AGO AND MY

FIRST YEAR IN PRO. FOOTBALL, I+CE 21.
COACH PHELAN WAS A CHARACTER
AND A CREATIVE COACH. WHILE IN J.C.;
I WENT DOWN TO LOS ANGELES
AND WATCHED ST MARY'S PRE-FLIGHT
PLAY A GAME. THE ATTRACTION WAS
COACH PHELAN'S CREATIVE OFFENSE — THEY
REALLY HAD RAZZLE-DAZZLE — LTS of
REVERSE TYPE RUNNING FOOTBALL. COACH
PHELAN AND I HAD A MUTUAL INTEREST IN
THE OUTDOORS. HE ONCE HELD UP A BUS FULL
OF L.A. DON PLAYERS TELLING ME A BEAR
STORY IN ALASKA. BEST REGARDS, ED Henke

Craig-

1949 was a long time ago and my first year in pro football, age 21. Coach Phelan was a character and a creative coach. While in JC, I went down to Lost Angeles and watched St. Mary's pre flight play a game. The attraction was Coach Phelan's creative offense. They really had razzle-dazzle, lots of reverse type running football. Coach Phelan and I had a mutual interest in the outdoors. He once held up a bus full of L.A. Don players telling me a bear story in Alaska.

Best Regards,
Ed Henke

Edgar Edwin Henke was destined to go by Ed. He was born in Ontario, CA on December 13th, 1927. Henke attended the University Of Southern California and was drafted by the Washington Redskins in the thirteenth round of the 1949 National Football League Draft. Ed decided to join the Los Angeles Dons of the All-American Football Conference rather than the NFL's 'Skins. Henke competed at defensive end in eleven games for the Dons before the upstart AAFC was absorbed by the NFL. Henke headed north and played in Canada for the Winnipeg Blue Bombers in 1950 and was named Western Interprovincial Football Union All Star for the season. Ed was named WIFU All Star with the Calgary Stampeders in 1954. In between he played in the NFL for the 49ers and made the Pro

Bowl in 1951. Overall, Ed Henke played fourteen years of professional football.

Jimmy Phelan (1892-1974) was a quarterback for the University Of Notre Dame from 1915 through the first three games of the 1917 season. He was drafted into the United States Army Air Corps and was a pilot in France during World War I. After the war Phelan embarked on a coaching career that would span three decades. He was the head coach at four colleges: University of Missouri, Purdue University, University of Washington and St. Mary's College. He had a record of 137 wins, 87 losses and 14 ties. For his excellence in coaching in the college ranks Phelan was inducted into the College Football Hall Of Fame in 1972. Coach Phelan's three seasons in the professional ranks were not quite as successful. He had a 12 and 26 record with the Dons and the Texans.

Bill Carpenter on playing for coach Earl Blaik:

Craig,

Sorry for the delay in responding to your recent request

Having the good fortune to play football for coach Blaik was a wonderful experience. He was much more than a coach; he was a great teacher and educator. Under him and on Army's playing field, I learned extremely valuable lessons about the value of hard work, sacrifice, teamwork, etc. Aside from my parents, his example, influence, and coaching probably had the greatest impact on my life.

Appreciate your interest,

Bill Carpenter

Craig,

Sorry for the delay in responding to your recent request.

Having the good fortune to play football for Coach Blaik was a wonderful experience. He was much more than a coach; he was a great teacher and educator. Under him and in Army playing field. I learned extremely valuable lessons about the value of hard work, sacrifice, teamwork, etc. Aside from my parents, his example, influence and coaching probably had the greatest impact on my life.

Appreciate your interest, Bill Carpenter

William Stanly Carpenter Jr. was born on November 30, 1937 in Springfield, PA. His father, William Sr., a United States Army infantryman and was killed in action in Germany toward the end of World War II.

Bill followed his father's footsteps and enrolled at United States Military Academy at West Point. While there he played end on the same squad as Heisman Trophy winning half back Pete Dawkins. Carpenter was known as the "Lonesome End" as he lined up toward the sideline similar to a modern day wide receiver. The 1958 West Point squad went undefeated. The following season Carpenter was the team captain and was named

a consensus All-American. He was inducted into the College Football Hall Of Fame in 1982.

After graduating from the Military Academy, Carpenter served bravely in Viet Nam where he earned a Silver Star and a Distinguished Service Cross. He retired as a lieutenant general.

Earl "Red" Blaik (1897-1989) played college football at Miami Of Ohio for two seasons before going to West Point for his final two seasons. In 1919 he was named All-American. After his playing days Blaik served in the Army for two years. Blaik was an assistant coach for several seasons before landing a head coaching job at Dartmouth in 1934. He coached there through 1940, at one point leading his team to a 22 game winning streak. Blaik became the head coach at West Point in 1941. During his 18 seasons coaching Army he led them to three consecutive National Titles from 1944 through 1946. Three of his charges won the Heisman Trophy and many of his assistant coaches went on to become successful head coaches including Sid Gilman and Vince Lombardi.

Blaik once referred to Bill Carpenter as "the greatest end I ever coached at West Point."

Fred Morrison on George Halas:

Craig

Coach Halas was a truly Great inspiration to Hundreds of Players who were fortunate enough to have been able to play for him and his Chicago Bears.

In 1950 I was a 1st round draft Choice of the Bears.

In 1950 we were 9 an 3 - we Beat the LA Rams twice But lost our last Game to the Chicago Cardinals That Put us in a tie with Rams and we lost to them in a playoff Game in L.A.

Coach Halas was inspirational to all of US. He was a Very Good + Fair man to all of US.

I wish the NFL had more Owners like Him today!

I also Played on 2 world Championship Teams with the Cleveland Browns in 1954 & 1955

Chi Bears #15 1950, 51, 52, & 53
Cleveland Browns #32 1954, 55 & 56

Fred "Curly" Morrison

211

Craig,

Coach Halas was a truly great inspiration to hundreds of players who were fortunate enough to have been able to play for him and his Chicago Bears.

In 1950 I was a 1st round draft choice of the Bears.

In 1950 we were 9 and 3. We beat the LA Rams twice but lost our last game to the Chicago Cardinals. That put us in a tie with Rams and we lost to them in a playoff game in LA.

Coach Halas was inspirational to all of us. He was a very good and fair man to all of us. I wish the NFL had more owners like him today!

I also played on 2 World Championship teams with the Cleveland Browns in 1954 & 1955.

Chicago Bears #15 1950, 51, 52 & 53

Cleveland Browns #32 1954, 55 & 56

Fred "Curly" Morrison

Fred Lew Morrison was born in Columbus, Ohio on October 7th, 1926. He stayed home for his college career playing for the Ohio State Buckeyes. "Curly" began as an end on offense and led the Buckeyes in receptions with seven. Morrison moved to fullback for his junior and senior seasons. His senior season he scored nine touchdowns to lead the team.

Curly Morrison capped off his college career in style. The 1950 Rose Bowl featured the heavily favored University Of California Bears versus Morrison's Buckeyes. In front of 101,000 fans in Pasadena, Morrison carried the ball 24 times for 127 yards and a touchdown. The Buckeyes won 17-14 and Morrison was named the 1950 Rose Bowl Most Valuable Player.

The Chicago Bears tabbed Fred Morrison with the 10th overall pick in the 1950 NFL Draft. In four seasons with Halas' Bears, Morrison ran for over a thousand yards and scored six rushing touchdowns. He also handled the punting duties.

1954 brought Curly back to his native Ohio. Paul Brown worked a trade to bring the former Buckeye star to his Browns. The trade paid dividends as the Browns won the NFL Championship in 1954 and 1955. 1955 was the most productive statistical season of Morrison's career. That season he carried the ball 156 times for 824 yards and three touchdowns. He made his first and only Pro Bowl for his performance. Morrison retired from the NFL after the 1959 season.

After his retirement Morrison became the first former player to become an announcer for CBS. He handled the color commentary for Browns games on the CBS Sports Sunday Spectacular program. Morrison played an integral role in Art Modell purchasing the Browns in 1961.

Dick Vermeil on *Invincible*:

CRAIG. I WAS VERY NERVOUS ABOUT IT AT FIRST. AFTER I SAW
THE MOVIE, I THOUGHT THEY DID A GOOD JOB. MY EX-PLAYERS
SAID I WAS MUCH MORE INTENSE THAN THE MOVE SHOWED ME TO BE.
BEST TO YOU. THANK YOU FOR YOUR INTEREST.

RETIRED COACH. Dick Vermeil

Craig Sievers

Craig, I was very nervous about it at first. After I saw the movie I thought they did a good job. My ex-players said I was much more intense than the movie showed me to be. Best to you. Thank you for your interest.

Retired Coach, Dick Vermeil

Greg Kinnear as Dick Vermeil

Richard Albert Vermeil was born in Calistoga, California on October 30, 1936. Dick attended San Jose State University and was a backup quarterback for the Spartans. He went into coaching immediately upon graduation in 1959. From 1959 through 1975 Vermeil was an assistant or head coach at every level. He was a head coach at the high school, junior college and major college level. In 1969 Vermeil was hired

Dick Vermeil as himself

by Pro Football Hall Of Fame coach George Allen as the first special teams coach in the National Football League. After his tenure with Allen's Los Angeles Rams coach Vermeil took the head coaching job at the UCLA. In 1975 he led the Bruins to a Rose Bowl win over top ranked Ohio State.

Vermeil began his NFL coaching tenure in 1976 with the Philadelphia Eagles. He coached seven seasons in Philadelphia, four of them being winning seasons. In 1980 he led the Eagles to a 12-4 record and a match-up with the Oakland Raiders in Super

Bowl XV. The Raiders won 27-10. Vermeil would retire for the first time after the 1982 season.

After a decade and a half hiatus Vermeil took the head coaching job with the St. Louis Rams. His first two seasons were forgettable with a combined 9-23 record. The 1999 season started disastrously. Vermeil's starting quarterback, Trent Green, went down with a serious knee injury during the preseason. That left him with no option but to start Kurt Warner at quarterback. Warner went from undrafted unknown to Super Bowl MVP. Vermeil retired again after his Super Bowl XXXIV victory.

His retirement only lasted a year as Vermeil took the head coaching job with Kansas City. In five seasons with the Chiefs he had an 80-44 record. Coach Vermeil retired from coaching for presumably the last time in 2005. His post football time has been spent pursuing his longtime passion; fine wine.

Invincible starred Greg Kinnear as Dick Vermeil and Mark Wahlberg as Vince Papale. The movie is based on Papale's journey from tending bar to playing in the National Football League.

Mick Tingelhoff on coach Bud Grant:

Hi Craig,

 Bud Grant was the smartest man I ever met. He knew Football inside + out. Nobody could say a bad word. He would get mad and tell you to grow up. NO drinking any beer either. Not good For you, just a great guy and great coach.

 Mick Tingelhoff

Hi Craig,

Bud Grant was the smartest man I ever met. He knew football inside & out. Nobody could say a bad word. He would get mad and tell you to grow up. No drinking any beer either. Not good for you. Just a great guy and a great coach.

Mick Tingelhoff

MICK TINGELHOFF
MINNESOTA VIKINGS   CENTER

Henry Michael Tingelhoff was born in Lexington, Nebraska on May 22, 1940. Mick played his college football at the University Of Nebraska. He did not start at center until his senior season with the Cornhuskers. That 1961 season was a three win season in Lincoln and while Tingelhoff was a co-captain and played well he was not an all Big Eight or All American nominee. He did manage to play in two post season bowls.

The NFL Draft was a 20 round affair in 1962. The AFL Draft was comprised of 34 rounds. No team in either league saw fit to pick Mick Tingelhoff. Minnesota gave him a shot, signing him as an undrafted free agent. It turned out to be a very fortuitous decision for the NFL's Vikings. Tingelhoff took over the starting center position during his rookie campaign and would not relinquish his post until after the 1978 season.

During his 17 seasons in the trenches for the Vikings, Tingelhoff was named All Pro five straight seasons and was elected to six Pro Bowls. He also started in all four of Minnesota's appearances in the Super Bowl.

Bud Grant's (1927-) coaching career began immediately after his playing career ended. The Winnipeg Blue Bombers of the Canadian Football League named Grant head coach due to his ability to make offensive and defensive adjustments during his playing days with them. He led Winnipeg to four Grey Cups Championships in ten seasons. In Minnesota, Grant took over after Norm Van Brocklin was let go as head coach 1967. 12 winning seasons and four Super Bowl appearances later, Grant stepped down to focus on his love of the outdoors. He is a member of the Pro Football and Canadian Football Halls Of Fame.

Ed Meador on George Allen:

Craig

I think George Allen was the best football coach I ever played under, having played under a total of 4 coaches with the Rams. He was 110% business and he kept us enthused about the game.

He just was the greatest!

Thanks
E Meador #21
L A Rams 1959-70

Craig,

I think George Allen was the best football coach I ever played under, having played under a total of 4 coaches with the Rams. He was 110% business and he kept us enthused about the game.

He just was the greatest!

Thanks,

Ed Meador #21

LA Rams 1959-1970

ED MEADOR
LOS ANGELES RAMS   HALFBACK

Eddie Doyle Meador was born on August 10, 1937 in Dallas, TX. Ed began his love affair with football early in his life. He started playing organized ball during his seventh grade year in school and continued through his freshman year of high school. Unfortunately for his football career, Eddie's parents moved the family several times between the end of his freshman year and his junior year. Finally, his family settled down in Russellville, AR. At Russellville High in 1955, Meador was All State in football and also lettered in basketball and track.

Meador wanted to return to his home state of Texas to play football and to go to college. He went to Texas A&M where the legendary Paul "Bear" Bryant was the head coach. Unfortunately, Meador never got an audience with coach Bryant. Bear's staff told Meador that he was too small and that he would never play Division I football in the Southwest Conference. He took a chance on the University Of Tulsa but got the same reaction there. Not to be deterred, Meador headed back to Russellville and Arkansas Tech University. Eddie starred at tailback, cornerback and returner for the Wonder Boys. After his senior year, Meador was invited to play in the Optimist Bowl that pitted small school stars against the best players in Division I. While Meador's team was narrowly beaten by the D-I stars, he was named MVP of his team and caught the eye of pro scouts.

The Los Angeles Rams took a chance on the small school product and drafted him in the seventh round of the 1959 NFL Draft. The Rams were immediately rewarded for their selection. From 1959 to 1970 Meador starred in the defensive backfield for Los Angeles. He was named to eight Pro Bowl rosters, All Pro six times and All Western Conference seven times. He was named to the NFL All Decade Team for the 1960's. There is a grassroots effort to get Meador nominated to the Pro Football Hall Of Fame by the Veteran's Committee.

Bob Livingstone on Frank Leahy:

Dear Craig:

I am 90 years old and It hard to bring back the times. But Craig Leahy was one of the best of the time.

I thought he was great. On and off the field.

The best in life to you Craig and many happy days

B. Livingstone

Dear Craig:

I am 90 years old and it's hard to bring back the times. But Craig, Leahy was one of the best of the time.

I thought he was great. On and off the field.

The best in life to you Craig and many happy days,

Bob Livingstone

Robert Edward Livingstone was born in Hammond, IN on May 11, 1922. After earning varsity letters in basketball, baseball and football at Hammond High in 1939 and 1940, Livingstone travelled roughly 70 miles east to South Bend, IN and the University Of Notre Dame. By the beginning of the 1942 season it was obvious that there was going to be a military draft. Livingstone enlisted in the Army so that he could finish his sophomore season. Finish it he did as he was a contributing member of The Fighting Irish's National Championship squad in 1942.

Livingstone spent two and a half years in the South Pacific fighting from the Philippines to New Guinea. Bob returned stateside after the war ended and like so many GIs he faced decisions. The Chicago Bears had drafted him with pick 225 of the 1945 National Football League Draft. Rather than join the professional ranks Livingstone decided to return to South Bend to play out his college eligibility and earn his degree.

It turned out to be a fortuitous decision for Livingstone and for Notre Dame. Bob was a main cog in Coach Frank Leahy's offense. The Fighting Irish won the National Championship in

1946 and 1947. In the 1947 matchup against The University Of Southern California, Livingstone had a record setting 92 yard touchdown run. That mark still stands more than 65 years later.

With an honorable discharge and three National Championships under his belt, Livingstone took a job with the Chicago Rockets of the All American Football Conference. He played with the Rockets, Buffalo Bills, and the Chicago Hornets before the AAFC disbanded in 1949. Bob played one season for the original Baltimore Colts before they folded after one season in the NFL. The Chicago Cardinals drafted Livingstone in 1951 but he decided to call it a career.

Carroll Dale on Vince Lombardi:

Craig,

Coach Lombardi was a great coach to play for:

#1 He shot straight with the players, you knew where you stood, He did not jerk players around

#2 He was demanding, but the players knew that his demands were for the good of the team

#3 He chewed butt when <u>we won</u> and made corrections when we lost- but was careful- most coaches chew butt we the team loses and everything is great when you win- - Coach Lombardi chewed when you didn't feel he was blaming you for a loss-

Carroll Dale
#84

Craig,

Coach Lombardi was a great coach to play for:

#1 He shot straight with the players, you knew where you stood, he did not jerk players around

#2 He was demanding, but the players knew that his demands were for the good of the team.

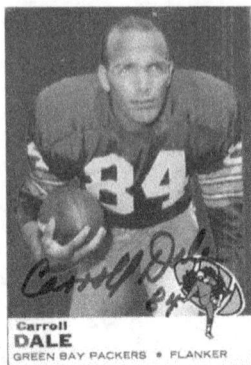

Carroll
DALE
GREEN BAY PACKERS • FLANKER

#3 He chewed butt when <u>we won</u> and made corrections when we lost but was careful. Most coaches chew butt when the team loses and everything is great when you win. Coach Lombardi chewed when you didn't feel he was blaming you for a loss.

Carroll Dale #84

In the city of Wise in the state of Virginia Carroll Wayne Dale was born on April 24, 1938. Dale traveled three hours east to attend Virginia Tech in Blacksburg. In 1956 Dale began his streak of 39 straight varsity starts as an offensive end. He led the team in receptions in each of his four seasons with the team. After his junior season Dale was named the Southern Conference Player Of The Year and also earned Second Team All-America honors. As a team captain his senior season, Dale continued his excellent play and was named a First Team All All-American. For his career at Tech Carroll Dale had 67 receptions for 1,195 yards and 15 touchdowns.

85 picks passed in the 1960 NFL Draft before the Los Angeles Rams picked Carroll Dale. Dale played 65 games during five seasons for the Rams. He used his speed to be the deep

threat receiver hauling in 149 passes for 2663 yards. Dale scored 17 touchdowns as a Ram and averaged almost 18 yards a catch.

That high average per catch caught the eye of Vince Lombardi. Baylor University's Larry Elkins was Green Bay's first round draft pick in 1965 and looked to be the answer as a speedy receiver for the Packers. Elkins was also drafted by the Houston Oilers of the AFL and he decided to stay in Texas. The Rams needed a linebacker so Green Bay sent Dan Currie to LA in exchange for Dale in a rare player-for-player NFL trade. The trade was a fortuitous one for the Green Bay. Dale went on to three Pro Bowls and contributed heavily to three Championship Packer teams.

Tony Nathan on Bear Bryant:

Coach Bear, was a Father for all who played for him. He believed in Gods Family. He made we write letters to our <u>Moms</u>!!! & go to church on Sundays.
But during the week we worked very hard to be the best we could be.

Tony Nathan 22
"75-78"

> *Coach Bear was a father for all who played for him. He believed in God & family. He made us write letters to our moms!!! & go to church on Sundays.*
>
> *But during the week we worked very hard to be the best we could be.*
>
> *Tony Nathan #22*
> *"75-78"*

Tony Curtis Nathan was born on December 14, 1956 in Birmingham, AL. He was a four sport star at Woodlawn High School lettering in baseball, basketball, track and football. For his prowess on the gridiron Nathan earned an athletic scholarship to the University Of Alabama. In 1978 Nathan was a team captain for Bear Bryant's squad that lost only one game and earned a trip to the Sugar Bowl. The New Year's Day match up with a one-

loss Penn State Nittany Lions team became an instant classic. The Crimson Tide rolled to a dramatic 14-7 victory with Nathan contributing 127 total yards to the cause. The victory brought a split National Championship to Tuscaloosa, the fifth title of Bryant's career. The Miami Dolphins drafted Nathan in the third round of the 1979 NFL Draft and were immediately rewarded as he was named All Pro his rookie season. Nathan would go on to play nine seasons for the Dolphins including Super Bowls XVII and XIX. After his playing career concluded Nathan went in to coaching in the college ranks and the NFL.

Paul "Bear" Bryant (1913-1983) attended the University Of Alabama and played for the football team from 1933 through 1935. He considered himself the "other end" as he played opposite of All-American and future Hall Of Famer Don Hutson. After graduation Bryant was drafted by the Brooklyn Dodgers in the fourth round of the 1936 NFL Draft but rather than continue his playing career he went immediately into coaching. He was an assistant coach with his alma mater, coached teams in the Navy during WWII, and was the head coach for one season at the University Of Maryland. Bryant then had successful stints at the University Of Kentucky and Texas A&M before returning to Tuscaloosa. During his quarter decade tenure as head coach at Alabama Bryant's teams won six National Championships.

Duane Putnam on Sid Gillman:

Craig,

Thanks for your letter I am 84 so my mind has to reload a little bit. In 1955 Sid - Coach Gilman came to Rams from Cincy. It took him a little bit of time to get up to speed with Pro's, but he caught on fast. It was pleasure to play for Coach Gilm and his Asst. Joe Madro - very good time in my life.

Bast of luck with endown Would like to see the end resuet,

Duane Putnam
L. A. Rams # 61

Craig,

Thank you for your letter. I am 84 so my mind has to reload a little bit.

In 1955 Sid- Coach Gillman came to Rams from Cincy. It took him a little bit of time to get up to speed with pros, but he caught on fast. It was pleasure to play for coach Gillman and his Asst. Joe Madro- very good time in my life.

Best of luck with endeavor, would like to see the end result.

Duane Putnam

L.A. Rams #61

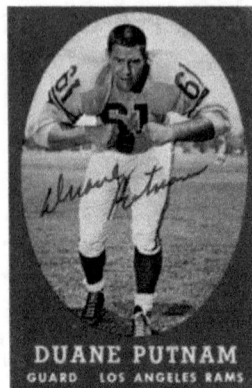

DUANE PUTNAM
GUARD   LOS ANGELES RAMS

Charles Duane Putnam was born in Pollack, South Dakota on September 5th, 1928. He was chosen by the Los Angeles Rams out of the College of Pacific in the 6th round of the 1952 NFL Draft. Putnam manned the offensive guard position for a decade in the National Football League. For his work during five consecutive seasons starting in 1954 he was voted to the Pro Bowl. Putnam was named First Team All Pro in 1955, '57 and '58. In 1960 Putnam was taken by the new Dallas Cowboys franchise in the expansion draft. He played one season each with the Cowboys and the Cleveland Browns before wrapping up his playing career with one last season with the Rams. Putnam spent several seasons with different NFL teams as an assistant coach.

Sid Gillman (1911-2003) played college football at Ohio State University. An encounter on the field with Bronko Nagurski during the first College All Star Game changed Gillman's career direction. Getting flattened by the Bears fullback led Sid to leave the gridiron and man the sideline instead. Gillman coached in the college ranks and had an 81 win 19 loss and 2 tie record over ten seasons. He then took his winning philosophies to professional football. Beginning in 1955 with Duane Putnam's LA Rams Gillman was a head coach the NFL and AFL for 18 seasons. He used his offensive innovations to lead teams to 12 .500 or better seasons and an AFL Championship with the Chargers in 1963. Gillman was inducted into the Hall Of Fame in 1983.

Bill McColl on George Halas:

Craig

George Halas was a great coach
but even a greater man — He was
interested in winning games but
even more interested in his
players future. After I quit the
Bears after 8 years to finish
my medical training — I went
to Korea for 2 years to work
as a Presbyterian medical missionary
in a leprosy hospital and George
Halas was my biggest supporter
Best Wishes
Bill McColl

Craig

George Halas was a great coach but even a greater man- He was interested in winning games but even more interested in his players future. After I quit the Bears after 8 years to finish my medical training- I went to Korea for 2 years to work as a Presbyterian Medical Missionary in a leprosy hospital and George Halas was my biggest supporter.

Best Wishes,
Bill McColl

William Frazer McColl Jr. was born on April 2, 1930 in San Diego, CA. He grew to be an incredible prep school athlete lettering in four sports while at Hoover High. With his rare combination of size and speed, McColl was offered football scholarships by colleges on the west coast and across the country. Bill instead took his 6' 4" 225 lb. frame to Stanford University on an academic scholarship.

On the field for the Stanford Indians (now known as the Cardinal) McColl's play at offensive end earned him consensus All-America honors after both his junior and senior years. He finished fourth in the voting for the 1951 Heisman Trophy. In the summer of 1952 McColl teamed with future Pro Football Hall Of Famers Frank Gifford, Ollie Matson, Hugh McElhenny and Gino Marchetti in the 19th Annual All Star Game in Chicago. The game featured the country's best college seniors pitted against the NFL's Champion from the previous season. The 1951 Champions were the Los Angeles Rams featuring HOFers Bob

Waterfield, Norm Van Brocklin, Dick "Night Train" Lane, Andy Robustelli, Tom Fears and Elroy "Crazylegs" Hirsch. The pros escaped the ameteurs that day by a field goal. For his exploits at Stanford McColl was inducted into the College Football Hall Of Fame in 1973.

Taken in the third round of the 1952 NFL Draft, McColl would go on to be a mainstay with the Chicago Bears for eight seasons. He was one of the first offensive ends to be used close to the formation as George Halas was in the process of popularizing the use of the tight end. During his tenure with the Bears McColl studied at The University Of Chicago and became an orthopedic surgeon. After he returned from Korea Bill McColl had a successful medical career and also chaired American Leprocy Missions Inc. He served on many boards including the Stanford Board of Trustees. McColl dabbled in politics running thrice for US Congress.

Tony Dungy on lessons from Chuck Noll:

1. Champions do the ordinary things better than everyone else.

2. Look for self motivated people.

3. Treating people fairly doesn't always mean treating everyone the same.

4. Help others be the best that they can be

5. Be stubborn in your convictions
   If you know something is right, don't compromise

Tony Dungy

Craig Sievers

1. Champions do the ordinary things better than everyone else

2. Look for self motivated people.

3. Treating people fairly doesn't always mean treating everyone the same.

4. Help others be the best that they can be.

5. Be stubborn in your convictions. If you know something is right don't compromise.

Tony Dungy

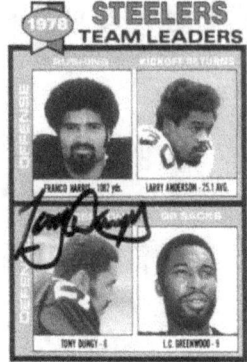

Jackson, MI welcomed Anthony Kevin Dungy on October 6, 1955. He played quarterback at the University Of Minnesota. He was passed over in the 1976 NFL Draft. Pittsburgh signed Dungy as a free agent and moved him to the defensive side of the ball. Playing safety, Dungy led the Steelers in interceptions during the 1978 campaign. Dungy earned a ring as a member of the Super Bowl XIII champion Steelers. His playing career came to a close after the 1980 preseason and he went immediately into coaching.

Dungy coached defensive backs at his alma mater during the 1980 season. The following season Chuck Noll tapped his former player to coach his defensive backs. Dungy was promoted to defensive coordinator of the Steelers in 1984. He would go on to coach defense in Kansas City and Minnesota through the 1995 season.

On January 22, 1996 Tampa Bay Buccaneers general manager Rich McKay gave Tony Dungy a shot at head coach.

Under Dungy's watch, the Buccaneers went from a laughing stock to a playoff team in the span of four seasons. Dungy found out that his success had created expectations as he was fired by Bucs owner Malcolm Glazer after losing in the 2001 Wild Card round.

Tony Dungy was unemployed for eight days before he signed with the Indianapolis Colts. The Colts boasted a prolific offense with quarterback Peyton Manning. It was the team defense that had held them back. He implemented his "Tampa 2" defense and tinkered with the roster. All his hard work culminated on February 4th, 2007 as his Colts won Super Bowl XLI.

Leo Sanford on Joe Stydahar:

Craig:

Coach Joe Stydahar was a alltime all pro playing for the Chicago Bears. He was really a great player and coach. He coached the Los Angeles Rams to a NFL world championship about 1951-52. He came to the Chicago Cardinals as a head coach in 1953 - 1955:

1 - He was a fine man and person to players.
2 - He knew football but should have brought in better assistant coaches to help.
3 - He could make you want to play and do your best.
4 - We ended up good friends after he left the Cardinals.

Leo Sanford

#51 - Chicago Cardinals 1951-57

#55 - Baltimore Colts 1958-59
        NFL World Champions
            1958 + 1959
    same as winning today Super Bowl!

Craig:

Coach Joe Stydahar was a all time All Pro playing for the Chicago Bears. He was really a great player and coach. He coached the Los Angeles Rams to a NFL World Championship about 1951-52

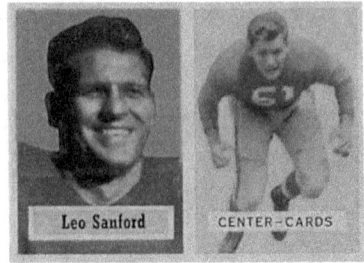

He came to the Chicago Cardinals as a head coach in 1953-1955;

1-He was a fine man and person to play for.

2-He knew football but should have brought in better assistant coaches to help.

3-He could make you want to play and do your best.

4-We ended up good friends after he left the Cardinals

> *Leo Sanford*

#51- Chicago Cardinals 1951-57

#55 Baltimore Colts 1958-59

NFL World Champions 1958 & 1959

Same as winning today's Super Bowl!

Ottis Leo Sanford was born on September 4th, 1929 in Dallas, TX. Leo was born in Texas but he grew up in Shreveport, Louisiana. After his prep career at Fair Park High in Shreveport Sanford had scholarship offers from several schools including Florida, LSU and Louisiana Tech. He chose Tech to the coaching staff and for the proximity to Myrna, the future Mrs. Leo Sanford. Sanford played center on offense and linebacker on defense helping Louisiana Tech to two Gulf States Conference championships. After his career with the Bulldogs, Sanford was chosen in the eighth round of the 1951 NFL Draft by the Chicago Cardinals. After seven seasons including two Pro Bowl nods Chicago traded Sanford to the Baltimore Colts before the 1958 season. That Colts team would go on to win the NFL Championship. The 1958 Championship is called "The Greatest Game Ever Played" and would be the last game Sanford's career.

"Jumbo Joe" Stydahar (1912-1977) was the sixth overall pick by the Chicago Bears in the 1936 draft. The 1936 draft was the very first National Football League Draft. For the late 1930's Stydahar was considered massive at 6'4" and 233 pounds. The speed and power he possessed made him ideal for "Papa Bear" George Halas' physically overwhelming style of play. Stydahar was named an All-Star four times, All-Pro six times and was a member of four NFL Championship teams in Chicago. He retired as a player after the 1946 Championship game. The Los Angeles Rams named Stydahar as head coach for the 1950 season. He lead the talented Rams to the Championship in 1951. Stydahar did not fare as well with the Cardinals winning only three games over two seasons. He was inducted into the Hall Of Fame in 1967.

Dan Orlich on Curly Lambeau:

Dear Craig—

I played under coach Lambeau for just one year, 1949. He was replaced by Gene Ronzani in 1950 and was hired as the coach for the Chicago Cardinals (later the St. Louis Cardinals — now the Phoenix Cardinals). I remember very little about "Curly" except that he was a legend in Green Bay (and Wisconsin). I do recall he had a fierce dislike for Geo. Halas and the Chicago Bears, and considered a victory over them as a successful season. I'm sorry to say people nowadays relate the Packers to the Lombardi era, very few knowing that "Curly" was the founder and won more titles than Lombardi ever did.

Sorry I can't help you more, Craig, "Curly" coached from 1920 to 1949 and there are damn few of us left who played for him. Good luck in your quest —

Sincerely,
Dan Orlich — Packers - '49-'52

Dear Craig-

I played under coach Lambeau for just one year, <u>1949</u>. He was replace by <u>Gene</u> <u>Ronzani</u> in 1950 and was hired as the coach for the Chicago Cardinals (later the St. Louis Cardinals, now the Phoenix Cardinals) I remember very little about "Curly" except that he was a legend in Green Bay (and Wisconsin). I do recall he had a fierce dislike for Geo. Halas and the Chicago Bears, and considered a victory over them as a <u>successful</u> <u>season</u>. I'm sorry to say people nowadays relate the Packers to the Lombardi era, very few knowing that "Curly" was the <u>founder</u> and won more titles than Lombardi ever did.

Sorry I can't help you more, Craig; "<u>Curly</u>" <u>coached from</u> <u>1920</u> <u>to</u> <u>1949</u> <u>and</u> <u>there</u> <u>are</u> <u>damn few</u> of us left who played for him. Good luck in your quest.

Sincerely,

Dan Orlich- Packers '49-'52

Daniel E. Orlich was born in Chisholm, MN on December 21, 1924. He attended the University Of Nevada Reno and went on to be drafted in the eighth round of the 1949 National Football League Draft. Orlich spent 36 games over three seasons in Green Bay playing defensive end. In 1950 he recovered three fumbles and returned one for a touchdown. After his NFL tenure Orlich returned to Nevada and embarked on what would be a decades-long career in competitive trapshooting. In 1979 he was inducted into the American Trapshooting Association Hall Of Fame.

Earl Louis "Curly" Lambeau (1898-1965) played one season for legendary coach Knute Rockne at Notre Dame before an illness forced him to leave school. He returned to his hometown of Green Bay, WI and was offered $250 a month to work as a clerk at the Indian Packing Company. A year later Indian formed a company football squad and called it the Packers. Lambeau played ten seasons for the Packers. After his playing career he embarked on a 29 year tenure on the sidelines in Green Bay. During that time he popularized the forward pass and utilized it in his coaching strategies to win six NFL Championships.

Buddy Cockrell on Sammy Baugh:

TO Craig:

Sammy Baugh was the first inductee in to the Football Hall of Fame in Canton, Ohio.

He was the first player to throw the forward pass and made it a regular play.

He might be the smartest Coach I ever played for. He still holds some of the punting records today. Before practice he would punt 60 yards

I was elated when he called me and signed me with the N.Y. Titans. He was the most comical coach ever to play for. He taught me not to take life to serious, to enjoy what you do, because there will always be a tomorrow.

A coach, mentor and true friend. I was fortunate to know him.

Buddy Cockrell

259

To Craig:

Sammy Baugh was the first inductee in to the Football Hall of Fame in Canton, Ohio.

He was the first player to throw the forward pass and make it a regular play.

He might be the smartest coach I ever played for. He still holds some of the punting records today. Before practice he would put 60 yards.

I was elated when he called me and signed me with the NY Titans. He was the most comical coach ever to play for. He taught me not to take life too serious, to enjoy what you do, because there will always be a tomorrow.

A coach, mentor and true friend. I was fortunate to know him.

Buddy Cockrell

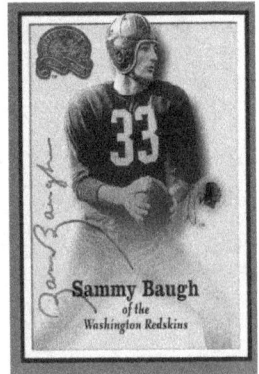

Gene "Buddy" Cockrell was born in Pampa, Texas on January 10, 1934. He played for the Oklahoma Sooners where he was a member of the undefeated 1955 National Championship team. In 1956 Cockrell transferred to Hardin-Simmons College in Abilene, Texas to compete in rodeo. He went to the National Finals Rodeo in 1956. Buddy did not give up football when he left Oklahoma. The coach of the Hardin-Simmons Cowboys was another actual cowboy, Sammy Baugh. Known as a gunslinger on the football field, Baugh competed in steer roping in Texas and even acted in the role of Tom King in *King Of The Texas Rangers*.

When Baugh became the coach of the New York Titans (later renamed the Jets) he contacted Cockrell, signed him and named him a team captain. Buddy played two years under Baugh in New York before hanging up his cleats for good in favor of his spurs. Cockrell went on to win the PRCA steer roping championship in 1977. Putting his business degree earned at Hardin-Simmons to good use, Buddy Cockrell owned and operated ranches around the world and even owned a mine in Costa Rica.

Charley Winner on Weeb Ewbank:

Craig,

When it comes to talking about Weeb Ewbank, I feel that I am more qualified than most people. I worked in the NFL for 37 years as a head coach, assistant coach and an administrator. Weeb was my college coach, my boss in the NFL with the Baltimore Colts, he was my father in law and a good friend.

Weeb was one of the best in football. He was a great teacher with a tremendous knowledge of football and people. He was very successful in high school, college and pro football and won on all three levels. He did not worry about the little things such as length of hair, dress code or back ground and race. He looked for character and dedication. Weeb could pick players who were self motivated and would work to get the job done. He would never overlook the smallest detail. His teams were always well prepared. He treated all players the same. The all pro or the free agent rookie receiving the same treatment. He believed in God and that is why he is coaching in heaven right now. He loved God and football.

Thank you for asking about Weeb,
He was great and good man. I
loved him.
Charley Winner.

263

Craig,

When it comes to talking about Weeb Ewbank, I feel that I am more qualified than most people. I worked in the NFL for 37 years as a head coach, assistant coach and an administrator. Weeb was my college coach, my boss in the NFL with the Baltimore Colts, he was my father in law and a good friend.

FRONT ROW: Rechlebar, Young, Spinney, Womble, Shula, Taseff, Taliaferro, Eggers, Matscheller, Dupre, Radik, Block, Trainer. 2nd ROW: Schuback, Equip. Mgr.; Marchetti, Donovan, Campanella, Joyce, Williams, Toth, Colteryahn, Pellington, Szymanski, Finnin, Myers, Langas. 3rd ROW: Winner, Coach; Cumiskey, Coach; Ewbank, Coach, Young, Kerkorian, Scarbath, Berry, McDonald, Potera, Bighead, Bretbauer, Evans, Marchetti, Sandusky, Lautar, Coach, Hughes, Coach. BACK ROW: Lesane, Shaw, Hugosian, Ameshe, Chorovich, Nutter, Vaughn, Jackson, Preas, Bryan, Bradshaw, Thomas.

Weeb was one of the best in football. He was a great teacher with a tremendous knowledge of football and people. He was very successful in high school, college and pro football and won on all three levels. He did not worry about the little things such as length of hair, dress code or background and race. He looked for character and dedication. Weeb could pick players who were self motivated and would work to get the job done. He would never overlook the smallest detail. His teams were always well prepared. He treated all players the same. The all pro or the free agent rookie receiving the same treatment. He believed in God and that is why he is coaching in heaven right now. He loved God and football.

Thank you for asking about Weeb.

He was a great and good man. I loved him.

Charley Winner.

Charley Winner was born on July 2nd, 1924 in Somerville, New Jersey. He served bravely in World War II flying B-17 Flying Fortress planes and was taken as a Prisoner Of War. Winner went on to play running back at Washington University

In St. Louis after he completed his military service. The Wash U. Bears were coached by Wilbur Charles Ewbank.

After his playing career Winner started what would be a long coaching odyssey. Winner took an assistant job with Case Tech Spartans, then joined Ewbank with the Baltimore Colts, stayed on with the Colts under Hall Of Famer Don Shula, was the head coach of the St. Louis Cardinals, joined Hall Of Famer George Allen with the Washington Redskins, rejoined Ewbank with the Jets, took over for Ewbank as the Jets head coach and wound up his coaching career as an assistant with the Cincinnati Bengals. For good measure, reuniting with Shula, Winner spent 11 seasons as the Director Of Player Personnel with the Miami Dolphins.

Rip Hawkins on Norm Van Brocklin:

Dear Craig,

Coach Van Brocklin was from the old school of
football. Not in knowing how the game was played, but
in how you as players should approch the game. He
was a great offensive analyst. He was a quarter back
when he played for the Eagles and he knew what
was necessary to make it work. He had very
little Tact when it came to the review of the
game on Mondays. You have to know that he
went into the Navy, before he played for the
Eagles. I liked him. He expected a lot out of
you and told you so. If he thought you were
giving your best, he accepted that. But don't
make excuses for mistakes and don't make
the same mistakes twice. I played defense
and he did not come into meeting very often. I
played 5 years for him and only once did
he yell at me for my play. We were playing
The Colts that 2nd year, Lenny Moore ran
an off tackle play for 20 yds and a Touch down.
Jim Parker 290 lbs offensive tackle and 5 yr
All pro is where Moore ran behind. I knew
where the play was going so I headed for the
spot before Moore got there. But Parker
saw me coming and cut me off. He actually
picked me up and set me on my butt. Well we
were coming off the field after the Touch down

Rip Hawkins continued:

And Van Brocklin was irate. He was cussing and calling everyone names including me and he finally asked me where I was when the play broke. I looked at him and said "on my ass coach on my ass." He looked back at me and never said another word. When we reviewed the game films on Monday as a Team, when they got to Moore Touchdown, it showed Panther picking me up and dragging me on my butt. Coach never said a word, he ran in back and over again on the film. He said looking at me, Panther is a good Tackle. He never again raised his voice to me or questioned what I did on the field for the rest of my career.

He loved football and his players, we just as a whole not strong in every position we needed to win a lot of games. After I left the team after 5 seasons we kept up with each other. I left because of a family sickness and never played again.

Coach's only problem was he wanted to be out there on the field to make it right. He loved the game as I did. I hope this helps you to know that most of the stories about him are probably true, but he fought for the team + players and expected us to do the same.

Dear Craig,

Coach Van Brocklin was from the old school of football. Not in knowing how the game was played, but in how you as players should approach the game. He was a great offensive analyst. He was a quarterback when he played for the Eagles and he knew what was necessary to make it work. He had very little tact when it came to the review of the game on Mondays. You have to know that he went into the Navy before he played for the Eagles. I liked him. He expected alot out of you and told you so. If he thought you were giving your best he accepted that. But don't make excuses for mistakes and don't make the same mistake twice. I played defense and he did not come into meetings very often. I played 5 years for him and only once did he yell at me for my play. We were playing the Colts that 2nd year, Lenny Moore ran an off tackle play for 20 yds and a touchdown. Jim Parker 290 lbs offensive tackle and 5 yr All Pro is where Moore ran behind. I knew where the play was going, so I headed for the spot before Moore got there. But Parker saw me coming and cut me off. He actually picked me up and set me on my butt. Well we were coming off the field after the touchdown and Van Brocklin was irate. He was cussing and calling everyone names including me and he finally asked me where I was when the play broke. I looked at him and said "on my ass coach on my ass." He looked back at me and never said another word. When we reviewed the game films on Monday as a team, when they got to Moore touchdown it showed Parker picking me up and dropping me on my butt. Coach never said a

word, he ran it back and over again on the film. He said looking at me, Parker is a good tackle. He never again raised his voice to me or questioned what I did on the field for the rest of my career.

He loved football and his players, we just as a whole not strong in every position. We needed to win a lot of games. After I left the team after 5 seasons we kept up with each other. I left because of a family sickness and never played again. Coach's only problem was he wanted to be out there on the field to make it right. He loved the game as I did. Hope this helps you to know that most of the stories about him are probably true, but he fought for the team and players and expected us to do the same.

Rip

Craig Sievers on Randy Gradishar:

I was probably eight years old at the time so that puts us around 1988. I was too young to have seen Gradishar play. I mainly knew about him from old highlight videos and from what I read on the back of football cards.

He was doing a signing at the community center in town so my buddy and I rode our bikes over there after school. We stood in line for a few minutes and then it was my turn. I remember being a little nervous. I had never met a famous person before.

I walked up and said "hello, sir." I handed him my two football cards and he signed them. When he was done he handed them back to me and put his hand out to shake. I shook his hand and to this day I remember how massive and mangled his hand was. I still have one of the cards.

Regards,

Craig.

Craig Sievers

CRAIG
SIEVERS

AUTHOR
AUBURN, NY

I was probably eight years old at the time so that puts us around 1988. I was too young to have seen Gradishar play. I mainly knew about him from old highlight videos and from what I read on the back of football cards.

He was doing a signing at the community center in town so my buddy and I rode our bikes over there after school. We stood in line for a few minutes and then it was my turn. I remember being a little nervous. I had never met a famous person before.

I walked up and said, "hello, sir". I handed him my two football cards and he signed them. When he was done he handed them back to me and put his hand out to shake. I shook his hand and to this day I remember how massive and mangled his hand was. I still have one of the cards.

Regards,

Craig.

Craig Sievers was born in Fort Collins, Colorado in 1980. In 1999 he was accepted to Colorado State University and after a year of studies, he left to fulfill his true passion as a craftsman. He moved to New York in 2004 and has resided in Auburn, NY since 2006. Sievers is an unwavering Denver Broncos fan has an almost encyclopedic knowledge of most sports trivia. In his free time, he enjoys playing golf when the Central New York weather permits, organizing his autographed card collection, and spending time at Downtown Books and Coffee in Auburn. Among all this, he has travelled throughout most of the United

States and Craig's passport is stamped by such countries as Vietnam, Honduras, Mexico, and Japan. Most days though, you can find him at home with his fiancé and their five fluffy children.

www.ingramcontent.com/pod-product-compliance
Lightning Source LLC
LaVergne TN
LVHW052017080426
835513LV00018B/2060